St. Pancras to Barking

J.E.Connor

Series editor Vic Mitchell

MP Middleton Press

Cover photograph : Ex-LMSR Class 4F 0-6-0 No. 44530 is seen passing Barking East signal box with the returning empty stock from a St. Pancras - Tilbury boat train in the 1950s. (H.C. Doyle / The Gresley Society)

First published November 2005

ISBN 1 904474 68 3

© Middleton Press

Cover design I P Graphics

Published by
   Middleton Press
   Easebourne Lane
   Midhurst, West Sussex
   GU29 9AZ
Tel: 01730 813169
Fax: 01730 812601
email : info@middletonpress.co.uk
www.middletonpress.co.uk

Layout and typesetting London Railway Record

Printed & bound by Biddles Ltd., Kings Lynn

INDEX

Barking	118	Junction Road Junction	38
Blackhorse Road	76	Kentish Town	17
Black Horse Road Goods	75	Leyton, Midland Road	92
Camden Road	15	Leyton, Midland Road Goods	97
Crouch Hill	49	Leytonstone High Road	98
East Ham	115	St. Ann's Road	67
Gospel Oak	29	St. Pancras	1
Harringay Green Lanes	59	South Tottenham	68
Harringay Park Junction	56	Upper Holloway	41
Highgate Road	35	Walthamstow Queen's Road	85
Highgate Road Junction	34	Walthamstow Q.R. (Goods)	91
Hornsey Road	48	Wanstead Park	105
Junction Road	39	Woodgrange Park	110

ACKNOWLEDGEMENTS

I should like to thank the various photographers, without whom this volume would not have been possible. I am also grateful to the small team of fellow researchers who kindly read the proofs, particularly my good friend, Geoff Goslin, who provided some useful additions to the text.

GEOGRAPHICAL SETTING

The route from St. Pancras climbs steeply up the northern slope of the lower Thames Valley and turns east at the south-east corner of Hampstead Heath. Gospel Oak station is on its boundary and is 150ft above sea level. The line is nowadays almost entirely in an urban area, but initially the western part was mostly rural.

East of Tottenham, the River Lea and Lea Navigation is crossed; adjacent to these are extensive reservoirs. A further six miles brings the route onto a bridge over the River Roding, on its approach to Barking.

The Channel Tunnel Rail Link Phase I runs roughly parallel to our route between St. Pancras and Barking. There is a massive ventilation shaft west of the latter station, as most of the line in underground.

All maps herein are to the scale of 25 ins to 1 mile and have north at the top.

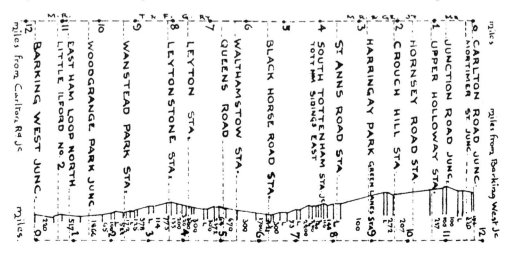

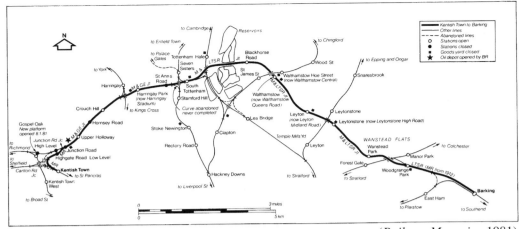

(*Railway Magazine* 1981)

HISTORICAL BACKGROUND

Looking at today's route linking Gospel Oak with Barking, it is perhaps difficult to imagine that at one time it hosted boat trains which plied between St. Pancras and Tilbury.

It owes its origins to a scheme of the early 1860s which was to provide a link between the Great Eastern Railway and Hampstead Junction Railway, along with a short connection to the Great Northern Railway near Hornsey.

The route was to leave the GER at Tottenham and join the HJR at the station then known as Kentish Town, but now named Gospel Oak. Its promoters hoped that it would attract London & North Western Railway goods traffic to and from the docks, but as there was already an existing link by way of the North London line, this seemed unlikely. The NLR and LNWR were closely associated with each other and saw the scheme as a possible threat, so the London & North Western gave it no encouragement.

Despite this however, the Bill for the Tottenham & Hampstead Junction Railway was placed before Parliament and received the Royal Assent on 28th July 1862, with the GER agreeing to operate it a month earlier.

The following year, the Midland Railway received authority to construct its London Extension and a connection between the two routes near Kentish Town was duly sanctioned. Over the years this was to prove particularly useful to the Midland and from the outset it provided a link with the London Docks.

A further Act, passed on 16th July 1866 permitted the Company to raise extra capital and authorised both the Midland and Great Eastern Railways to subscribe. At the same time the companies received powers by which they could take over the route and work it as a joint venture on terms that were to be agreed.

Work began on the THJR and completion was expected by the autumn of 1867. The route was inspected by Colonel Hutchinson of the Board of Trade on 24th June that year, but he was unhappy with the progress and refused permission to open. The junction with the HJR had yet to be made, although his report noted the lines were "laid close". Further inspections followed, but problems with both track and signalling resulted in a lengthy delay. Eventually the Board of Trade agreed to sanction opening, but only on the understanding that a 20mph speed restriction would be imposed until more robust rail chairs had been installed. In the meantime, the HJR had opened a new station to serve Kentish Town, so from 1st February 1867, the location of the future junction was renamed Gospel Oak.

On 21st July 1868 GER passenger trains began to operate over the route, but for the time being these terminated at Highgate Road, which was located 21 chains east of Gospel Oak.

An earlier scheme to provide a link with the Edgware, Highgate & London Railway in the vicinity of Crouch Hill had floundered, possibly because of a difference in levels of around 70 feet, but work on the GNR connection went ahead. This curve was referred to in the THJR Act of 1862 as 'Railway No.4', and was described at the time as providing "a junction with the main line of the

GNR 37 chains north of the bridge carrying Hornsey Wood Lane". The track had been laid by the time of Colonel Hutchinson's initial inspection, but, as at Gospel Oak, the junction itself had not been completed.

From a GNR source it seems that a connection of sorts may have been provided in April 1864, but removed five months later. Information is rather ambiguous, but if this indeed took place, it must have been only as a temporary measure during construction as track-laying on the THJR did not commence until sometime later. In fact, the connection was not to materialise for many years and, having become derelict, the curve had been lifted by 1881.

Originally, the only stations on the THJR were located at Crouch Hill, Upper Holloway and Highgate Road, as much of the route remained fairly rural at the time. MR freight traffic commenced on 3rd January 1870, but by then passenger receipts were already deemed disappointing. These were so low that they did not even cover operating expenses so the GER bowed to the inevitable and announced that from 31st January 1870 the passenger service would cease. With this move the future of the route looked far from bright, particularly as the Company's affairs were being administered under the Court of Chancery.

Passenger services were soon restored, but this time they were provided by the GER and the MR.

Once the connection at Kentish Town became a reality, the Midland Railway began using the THJR for its dock traffic instead of the North London line as before. To achieve this the Company reached an agreement with the GER whereby it could use its metals beyond Tottenham and, in return, allowed the Great Eastern to serve St. Pancras. At the time, the GER had to make do with its cramped, inconveniently sited terminus at Bishopsgate, as Liverpool Street had not yet been built. Therefore the possibility of using another terminus was extremely welcome.

Passenger figures began to improve and additional stations were opened at Junction Road and Hornsey Road on 1st January 1872. During that year the GER began operating over its new line from Hackney Downs to Edmonton and thence into Enfield. A spur off the THJR was to be added which would have allowed through running between Hackney Downs and St. Pancras, but although the embankment was built the link was never completed. In 1879 however, a connection between South Tottenham and Seven Sisters on the GER was brought into use for freight traffic, with passenger services commencing at the beginning of the following year.

By now the line which had started off so disastrously was beginning to show promise, so stations were opened at Green Lanes and St. Ann's Road on 1st June 1880 and 2nd October 1882 respectively. It seems that a degree of confusion occurred regarding Green Lanes, as there was already a station of that name on the GER Palace Gates branch, so in 1884 the THJR premises were renamed 'Harringay Park', although 'Green Lanes' was retained as a suffix. The two stations were actually some distance from each other, but the thoroughfare on which they stood was very lengthy. Explaining this in a 1919 edition of the *Railway Magazine,* H.L. Hopwood wrote: *"Green Lanes is the name of the main road that goes from Stoke Newington to Enfield, but as it extends for some miles, it is alternatively called the High Road of the particular district passed through, e.g., High Road, Wood Green, &c."*

On 2nd April 1883 the Midland Railway completed an east-facing connection from its main line which allowed through running between the industrial Midlands and the London Docks. This diverged at Carlton Road Junction, then, having passed in tunnel beneath both the HJR and the Kentish Town - Highgate Road line of 1870, ran at a lower level alongside the THJR before joining it near Junction Road.

The idea of a junction with the HJR at Gospel Oak had been opposed by the LNWR and NLR, as both companies wanted all traffic to and from the docks to use the North London line. The section of line west of Highgate Road therefore remained unused and presumably lay semi-derelict. After a while however the Joint Committee decided to open this stretch and extend passenger services to a single-platform at Gospel Oak, situated behind the up side of the HJR station. From the weekly notice issued at the time it is apparent that the opening took place on Sunday 27th May 1888, although GER passenger trains were not extended beyond Highgate Road until a week later on 4th June.

The next major development came during the following decade when train services were extended from South Tottenham to Barking and East Ham by way of the new Tottenham & Forest Gate Railway.

The line had been the brainchild of local property developer Thomas Warner, founder of the Warner Estate Company, and it received its Act of Incorporation on 4th August 1890. Again it was to be jointly managed, but this time the Midland was to be partnered by the London, Tilbury & Southend

Railway.

The TFGR commenced to the east of South Tottenham station, then continued to Woodgrange Park where it joined the original LTSR Barking - Forest Gate route of 1854. Passenger stations were to be located at Black Horse Road, Walthamstow, Leyton, Leytonstone and Forest Gate, with the possibility of one serving Lea Bridge Road, although the latter did not materialise. In addition, goods and coal yards would be provided at Black Horse Road, Boundary Road, Hainault Road and Royal Lodge.

From Black Horse Road to Boundary Road, Walthamstow, the line was to be in cutting, but the continuation towards Forest Gate would be carried largely on viaduct. Much of the area had already been developed by this time, so certain existing properties had to be acquired and demolished before work could start. This of course cost money and lack of the necessary finances resulted in construction being delayed. Work commenced in 1891 however and was completed within three years.

As part of the scheme, the LTSR subsequently agreed to provide a station on its own section of line at Woodgrange Park and issued a contract for it in 1893. Elsewhere various finishing touches were being made and prior to opening, the goods yards at Hainault Road, Royal Lodge and the passenger station at Forest Gate had been renamed as Leyton, Leytonstone and Wanstead Park respectively.

The TFGR was officially brought into use on 1st July 1894, although there was no booked services until the following day, when through goods trains, not stopping at the intermediate yards, were introduced between West End Sidings on the Midland Railway and Barking. Passenger services to East Ham and Southend followed a week later on 9th July and the intermediate yards eventually opened at the beginning of September.

Changes were also about to take place at the other end of the line, where an improved connection with the Midland was to be constructed. Around this time, the section of line between St. Paul's Road Junction and Kentish Town was being widened, so the opportunity was taken to provide a new link with the THJR. Until then, trains from St. Pancras or Moorgate Street had to cross the goods lines on the level at Kentish Town then climb at 1 in 48 before reaching the station at Highgate Road. The new spur was to diverge alongside Kentish Town locomotive depot then continue towards the existing low-level Carlton Road - Junction Road link, which it would join at Mortimer Street Junction. Known as the Kentish Town Curve, this

Public notice of 1891. (K. Romig collection)

had a much easier rising gradient of 1 in 110 and it was officially brought into use on 16th December 1900, with public services commencing the following day. A new Low Level station was provided at Highgate Road, which belonged solely to the Midland Railway, whereas the existing premises on the formation above were managed by the Joint Committee.

Since opening, the THJR had been worked by both the GER and Midland companies, but it did not actually belong to them. This was to change however following the Midland Railway Act of July 1902, when it officially became the Tottenham & Hampstead *Joint* Railway. Since 1885 the maintenance of the THJR line had been divided, the Midland being responsible as far as Crouch Hill tunnel, and the GER from there to Tottenham.

The first decade of the twentieth century saw the spread of electric tramways around London and these began to erode much of the line's local traffic. A look at some of the passenger figures for the period demonstrates only too clearly the way that receipts were dropping. In 1896 for example, 125,125 passengers had been booked at Junction Road, but by 1922 this had fallen to 30,251. A similar situated existed elsewhere on the line, such as at Hornsey Road, which during the same period dropped from 199,350 to 30,629. The section east of South Tottenham fared rather better, as indicated by the number of passengers booking at Leyton, which rose from 129,861 to 228,684.

It had seemed likely that the LTSR would be absorbed by a larger company. Of these, the most obvious contender was the GER, which also served the areas east of London and was also the possessor, at least on a 999 year lease, of Fenchurch Street station, which the LTSR used as its principal London terminus.

At the beginning of the twentieth century, various meetings were held between the GER and LTSR to discuss a possible takeover, but nothing was agreed. In 1910, an offer was made by the North London Railway, which by then was being worked by the larger LNWR, but this was not accepted. Around the same time, the Midland came forward and entered into a series of detailed discussions which eventually paid off. A Bill authorising the Midland take-over was placed before Parliament and was passed on 7th August 1912.

With the disappearance of the LTSR as an independent company, the Tottenham & Forest Gate line officially became the property of the Midland Railway, although very few, if any, changes appear to have been made to the various stations.

World War I however brought the inevitable reductions in facilities and resulted in both the High and Low Level stations at Highgate Road being permanently closed. Another change came at Gospel Oak, where the long-deferred junction between the THJR and Hampstead Junction line was finally laid and brought into use on 23rd January 1916. This was only intended as a temporary measure to allow through running of trains assisting the war effort and, having fallen into disuse, was removed on 3rd September 1922. The abandoned connecting curve at Harringay was brought back to life for the same reason, but was likewise soon abandoned and the junction with the GNR severed in 1920.

A little earlier, in 1919, H.L. Hopwood recorded that passenger trains over the THJR and TFGR were formed of Midland bogie stock, marshalled into sets of six vehicles, although in less busy times only four coaches were deemed necessary. Mr. Hopwood also stated that *"These trains replaced older close-coupled sets of 10 four-wheelers."* The same *Railway Magazine* article also referred to the curious duplication of mileposts on the section between South Tottenham and Junction Road. Those on the north side were original and indicated the distance from Tottenham North Junction and Gospel Oak, whilst those to the south dated from the opening of the TFGR and were measured from St. Pancras.

The railway grouping of 1923 saw the THJR come under the joint ownership of the London Midland & Scottish and London & North Eastern Railways, whilst the section east of South Tottenham was purely LMSR.

By then, the majority of trains operated over the Kentish Town route, whilst those serving the single terminal platform at Gospel Oak had been drastically reduced. They officially ceased altogether from September 1926, although traffic was restored on bank holidays and the odd special occasion until August 1939.

A few LMSR 'hawkseye' type nameboards began to appear on the route during the 1930s, but no more significant changes took place until World War II.

As with the previous global conflict, the war brought station closures, the casualties this time being Junction Road, Hornsey Road and St. Ann's Road. The Gospel Oak and Harringay connections

TOTTENHAM & HAMPSTEAD JOINT RAILWAY.

Instructions to be observed by the Signalman and Shunters on duty at Upper Holloway, respecting the use of the Bell fixed near the Shunters' Cabin, and worked from the Signal Box.

This Bell has been provided to enable you to intimate to the Shunters in the Sidings when it is necessary to clear the Main Line for other Trains to pass, and it must be used in accordance with the following instructions :—

Messenger required...   ...   . One Ring.
Clear Down Main Line for Passenger Train to ⎱ Two Rings.
pass   ...   . ⎰
Train on Up Main Line requiring to stop for ⎱ Three „
Traffic purposes...   ...   . ⎰

Should any breach of these Instructions occur, it must be immediately reported.

By Order.

February. 1906.

Operating notice of 1906. (K. Romig collection)

B R I T I S H   R A I L W A Y S.
(LONDON MIDLAND REGION).

INSTRUCTIONS TO SIGNALMEN AT HIGHGATE ROAD JUNCTION BOX,
KENTISH TOWN

The Absolute Block Regulations apply on the up and down
main lines between Junction Road Junction box, this box and
Gospel Oak Station box.

ABSOLUTE BLOCK REGULATIONS

Regulation 1.
Clause (e) of this regulation applies for trains on the
down main line.
The special Is line clear signal, 1-2-3, will be received
and must be sent on the down main line for freight trains
proceeding to Ferme Park via Harringay Park Junction.

Regulation 5.
Except during fog or falling snow, a train not conveying
passengers may be accepted from Gospel Oak Station box on
the down main line in accordance with this regulation,
provided the line is clear to a point opposite the up main
home signal and the line within the clearing point is not
occupied by a train or vehicle containing passengers.
This regulation is authorised, in clear weather and
during fog or falling snow, at Gospel Oak Station box on
the up main line for a train not conveying passengers.

Regulation 31.
This regulation is authorised from Junction Road Junction
box to this box on the up main line.

OTHER INSTRUCTIONS.

Rule 39 (b).
During fog or falling snow, a train must not be allowed
to draw to the up or down main starting signals to await
acceptance.

FOG MARKING POINT.
Up main starting signal.

Derby,
January, 1964.   *E. Cowell*
                                      LINE MANAGER.

BR memorandum of 1964. (D. Jones collection)

were reinstated however and, unlike before, were retained when hostilities ended.

At nationalisation in 1948, most of the route became part of the London Midland Region of British Railways, although the former TFGR section was transferred to the Eastern Region, along with the main ex-LTSR lines on 20th February 1949. The line between South Tottenham and Harringay was also part of the Eastern Region, with the LMR boundary believed to be just east of Crouch Hill.

The 1950s proved to be the last decade of steam operation. The stations themselves remained little changed and possessed a character that was all their own. Those on the viaduct section of the former TFGR were particularly memorable, with their wooden platform buildings and wide empty stairways which smelt of encroaching decay. Their distinctive forms somehow looked incongruous with the blue signs and faded cream and green paintwork given to them by the Eastern Region.

Well into the 1960s a number of the booking offices retained pre-nationalisation tickets for less-popular journeys and one of them even boasted luggage labels dating back to Midland days.

The local service was now largely restricted to operating between Kentish Town and Barking, because the section to East Ham closed in 1958.

The route continued to prove important for freight traffic and 1959 saw the completion of a flyover system at Barking which allowed workings from the Tilbury direction to pass above the Fenchurch Street and London Transport District Lines as they headed towards Woodgrange Park and beyond. During this period of modernisation, the line between Barking and Forest Gate Junction was provided with overhead wiring, but the rest of the route towards Kentish Town was not electrified.

Local goods traffic declined and the various yards closed during the 1960s. Rationalisation of passenger station buildings followed in the next decade and the line took on an even more derelict aspect. With the old structures gone, weeds began to break through the platform surfaces and the meagre replacement shelters did nothing to dispel the overall atmosphere of gloom.

In connection with the Bedford - St. Pancras electrification scheme, it was intended to divert Barking trains by way of the North Curve to Carlton Road Junction and thence into a bay at West Hampstead. Clearances for this were made at West Hampstead, but pathing difficulties through Belsize Tunnels resulted in them being routed into Gospel Oak instead. The remains of the abandoned platform, last used by passengers in 1939, was demolished and replaced by a new structure in readiness for the changeover which took place on 5th January 1981.

In June 1986, all lines within the London area, and in some cases well beyond, were incorporated into a new organisation called Network SouthEast. This disintegrated during the next decade following the railway privatisation scheme imposed by the Conservative government, which saw the responsibility of infrastructure passing to an organisation known as Railtrack, whilst services were sold off to various Train Operating Units. That which took over the Barking - Gospel Oak line along with the former NLR and LNWR suburban routes was named 'North London Railways', and trains began running under this banner from 1st April 1994. A further change came in September 1997 when services were re-launched as SilverLink Metro, whilst in 2003 Railtrack was replaced by Network Rail.

The Barking - Gospel Oak Line Committee, subsequently renamed The Barking - Gospel Oak Line User Group, was formed in the 1960s when the line appeared to be under threat, and ever since it has campaigned tirelessly for improvements.

When opened in 1868, the line was provided with six weekday trains which operated in both directions from Highgate Road to Fenchurch Street, along with one each way between Highgate Road and Stratford only, with a reduced service on Sundays, (although the short working from Stratford ran in one direction only).

In the summer of 1886, the GER introduced a through service between Highgate Road and Chingford, partly for the use of passengers wishing to visit Epping Forest. Twelve trains ran each way on weekdays, with a slight reduction on Sundays, and cheap return tickets encouraged their use. The weekday service was reduced to eight trains in each direction during the winter months and four on Sundays, although at this time of year there could have been little prospect of excursion traffic. In 1888 these workings were extended over the newly opened section to Gospel Oak. Probably the oddest working of this decade was a morning train from South Tottenham which, in 1883, ran through to Victoria by way of Kentish Town, the Metropolitan Widened Lines, Snow Hill and Loughborough Junction.

In 1892, the Great Eastern began to operate a through train between Gospel Oak and Southend-on-Sea on Summer Sundays only, but in the summer of 1895, this ran daily.

The opening of the Tottenham & Forest Gate Railway in 1894 brought additional through traffic when a service was introduced for the Summer between St. Pancras and Southend, with a few local trains subsequently turning back at Upminster. A fast Southend service was reintroduced (long term) in June 1895 and became established as four trains each way in the winter, plus extras in the summer (some of which ran to and from Kentish Town or stations on the T&H line, rather than to or from St. Pancras. For a while, these services were worked by Midland locomotives, with one being allocated to Shoeburyness specifically for the purpose. This arrangement ceased in April 1899, and from that date through services to and from St. Pancras were hauled by LTSR locomotives. The LTSR also operated trains between St. Pancras and Tilbury to connect with pleasure ships operated by New Palace Steamers Ltd.

The existence of the TFGR allowed the Midland Railway to extend its local trains from Moorgate Street and St. Pancras to East Ham in 1894 and, for some time, this was to be the principal passenger service over the route.

The T&H line also proved useful for certain GER main line trains which started or terminated at St. Pancras instead of Liverpool Street. It also saw royal patronage and was referred to in a 1919 edition of *The Railway Magazine* as *"The Royal Route"*, because it provided a convenient link between London and Sandringham. It seems that the 3.55pm weekday departure for Hunstanton, which had run since November 1886, operated during the Winter months *"for the convenience of the late Prince of Wales (afterwards King Edward VII) and his guests"*.

In July 1914 it was stated that sixty-two down and fifty-seven up Midland trains were using the route, along with twenty-three down and twenty-four up GER trains. Of the latter, sixteen in each direction were locals between Gospel Oak and Chingford, whilst the remainder were services between St. Pancras and the Cambridge line. An oddity of this period was the operation of

SEASON TICKET RATES WITH SOUTHEND.

	12 Months		6 Months		3 Months	
	1st class	3rd class	1st class	3rd class	1st class	3rd cl'ss.
	£ s. d.	£ s. d.	£ s. d.	£ s. d.	£ s. d.	£ s. d.
St. Pancras	28 12 9	20 0 0	14 8 6	10 0 0	7 3 0	5 0 0
Camden Road	28 6 0	19 10 6	14 3 6	9 15 6	7 1 6	4 18 0
King's Cross	28 12 0	20 0 0	14 6 0	10 0 0	7 3 0	5 0 0
Kentish Town	28 0 0	19 1 0	14 0 0	9 10 6	7 0 0	4 15 6
Highgate Road	28 0 0	19 1 0	14 0 0	9 10 6	7 0 0	4 15 6
Junction Road	27 14 0	18 11 6	13 17 0	9 6 0	6 18 6	4 13 0
Upper Holloway	27 14 0	18 11 6	13 17 0	9 6 0	6 18 6	4 13 0
Hornsey Road	27 14 0	18 2 0	13 17 0	9 1 0	6 18 6	4 10 6
Crouch Hill	27 8 0	18 2 0	13 14 0	9 1 0	6 17 0	4 10 6
Harringay Park	27 8 0	17 12 6	13 14 0	8 16 6	6 17 0	4 8 6
St. Ann's Road	27 2 0	17 3 0	13 11 0	8 11 6	6 15 6	4 6 0
South Tottenham	26 16 0	17 3 0	13 8 0	8 11 6	6 14 0	4 6 0

	2 Months		1 Month		2 Weeks		1 Week	
	1st cl'ss	3rd cl'ss	1st cl'ss	3rd cl'ss	1st cl'ss	3rd cl'ss	1st cl ss	3rd cl'ss
	£ s. d.	£ s. d.	£ s. d.	£ s. d.	£ s. d.	£ s. d.	£ s. d.	£ s. d.
St. Pancras	5 19 6	4 4 0	3 11 6	2 10 0	2 8 0	1 13 6	1 8 6	0 19 0
Camden Road	5 18 0	4 2 0	3 11 0	2 9 0	2 7 6	1 13 6	1 8 6	0 18 6
King's Cross								
Kentish Town	5 17 0	4 0 0	3 10 0	2 7 6	2 7 0	1 12 6	1 8 0	0 18 0
Highgate Road	5 17 0	4 0 0	3 10 0	2 7 6	2 7 0	1 12 6	1 8 0	0 17 6
Junction Road	5 15 6	3 18 0	3 9 6	2 6 6	2 6 6	1 11 6	1 7 6	0 17 6
Upper Holloway	5 15 6	3 18 0	3 9 6	2 5 6	2 6 6	1 11 0	1 7 6	0 17 0
Hornsey Road	5 15 6	3 16 0	3 9 6	2 5 6	2 6 6	1 11 0	1 7 6	0 17 0
Crouch Hill	5 14 6	3 16 0	3 8 6	2 5 6	2 6 0	1 11 0	1 7 0	0 17 0
Harringay Park	5 14 6	3 14 0	3 8 6	2 4 0	2 5 6	1 10 0	1 7 0	0 16 6
St. Ann's Road	5 13 0	3 12 0	3 8 0	2 3 0	2 5 6	1 9 0	1 7 0	0 16 0
South Tottenham	5 12 6	3 12 0	3 7 0	2 3 0	2 5 0	1 9 0	1 7 0	0 16 0

CONDITIONS.—Periodical tickets at half-price are issued to children under 15 years of age; they are also issued to scholars, students, apprentices, pupil teachers, articled clerks, learning a trade or profession, and junior clerks up to 18 years of age, on production of a certificate from the master of the school, the principal of the college, or their employer, as the case may be. A deposit of 10s. for each first class and 5s. for each third class ticket is also required, which will be returned if the ticket is given up immediately on expiration. If any periodical ticket is lost, upon the holder requires another to replace it, a new ticket will be issued upon payment of 10 per cent. upon the unexpired portion of the rate, the old deposit being forfeited and a fresh one charged.

On Saturday, August 2nd, Bank Holiday, August 4th, and Tuesday August 5th, certain booked trains will be withdrawn, of which due notice will be given by special bills at the stations.

Some of the luncheon and dining cars and through carriages which are announced in the Time-Tables will also be suspended on Bank Holiday, August 4th.

Season ticket rates, July - September 1902. (K. Romig collection)

through carriages between Southend and Derby. These were attached to the 10.45am Southend - St. Pancras train, then transferred to the 12.15pm departure for Liverpool. In the opposite direction they came up on the 9.15am Liverpool - St. Pancras (12.00 noon from Derby) then were attached to the 3.12pm train to Southend. This facility proved to be an early casualty of war, as it commenced operation in July 1914 but had ceased by 1915.

World War I economies resulted in all GER St. Pancras services being suspended and a reduction in the number of trains operating between Gospel Oak and Chingford. On the latter route there were now only two daily trains in each direction and one these turned back at Wood Street.

Services improved after the war ended, but the days of GER trains over the route were drawing to an end.

The LNER working timetable of 1923 shows what seem to be the last GE line main line trains to use St. Pancras. These were the 11.20am St. Pancras - Hunstanton and the 1.05pm Hunstanton - St. Pancras. These ran on Saturdays between 23rd July and 15th September inclusive and consisted of LNER stock, which worked empty to and from Tottenham.

The LNER finally withdrew its residual Gospel Oak - Chingford trains in 1926, leaving all regular passenger services over the line in the hands of the LMSR.

Initially the link with Barking was only used by through Southend-on-Sea services, whilst all local trains terminated in the bay at East Ham. From the early twentieth century, some of the MR local trains were diverted to Barking and this trend continued during the 1920s and 30s. The inter-war years also saw the reduction of through trains serving Moorgate Street, and these disappeared completely following the outbreak of hostilities in 1939. The St. Pancras - Southend service continued to operate however, although, as the war dragged on, it was reduced to just one train each way. After 1945, it reverted to the pre-war four trains in either direction, but further reductions were to follow.

For a number of years, the Midland and LMSR had operated boat trains from St. Pancras to Tilbury in connection with Orient Lines and P&O liners, and these continued into the BR era.

The local service now operated between Kentish Town and Barking or East Ham, although the latter was very much in decline. However, the construction of the Barking flyover and other engineering works in the vicinity resulted in the entire service being diverted to East Ham from 28th October 1957 until 14th September 1958, after which the link from Woodgrange Park was officially closed and all trains ran to Barking.

The St. Pancras - Southend through service was also in the process of petering out and ceased entirely in June 1962, on the introduction ex-LTSR line's new all-electric timetable. A loco-hauled train continued to make a return journey between Luton and Southend-on-Sea on Summer Sundays for a little longer, but this did not call at local stations and ceased completely after 1963.

Diesel multiple units commenced operating the Barking service in 1960 but, apart from a few early morning departures from St. Pancras, these all started from Kentish Town. The residual St. Pancras workings ended after an accident rendered Islip Street Junction signal box inoperative on 23rd December 1966.

The diversion of trains from Kentish Town to Gospel Oak in 1981 resulted in the service being increased from hourly to half-hourly and in 2005 the units working the route were well patronised.

Cover of BR leaflet issued April 1960 to publicise the new diesel services. (D. Jones collection)

ST. PANCRAS

1. Let us turn the clock back to the days when the line had a direct service from central London and start our journey at St. Pancras. The station was opened by the Midland Railway on 1st October 1868, although the Midland Grand Hotel, which formed the main frontage seen here, had yet to be built. Prior to construction, a competition was organised in 1865 and architects were invited to forward their proposed designs. The winner was Sir George Gilbert Scott, although his original scheme, which envisaged the uppermost floor being occupied by railway offices, was subsequently modified in the interests of economy. Work started on the hotel building in 1868, but progress was slow and it was not until 5th May 1873 that the first section was ready for occupation, with the completion of the west wing following three years later. Our view was taken from the south side of Euston Road and looks north-east. To the left we see Midland Road, with a section of the station's overall roof just visible in the distance, whilst on the extreme right is part of the frontage belonging to the Great Northern Railway terminus at King's Cross. The photograph, which dates from the dawn of the twentieth century, shows the 565 feet-long frontage and the impressive 270-ft high tower which featured a clock supplied by John Walker of Cornhill in 1872. (Commercial postcard / P. Laming collection)

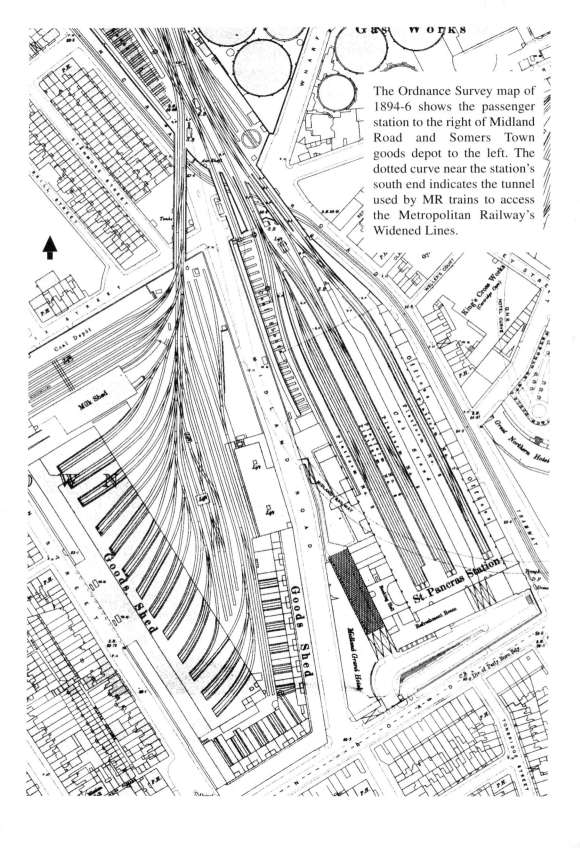

The Ordnance Survey map of 1894-6 shows the passenger station to the right of Midland Road and Somers Town goods depot to the left. The dotted curve near the station's south end indicates the tunnel used by MR trains to access the Metropolitan Railway's Widened Lines.

2. We now stand at the western corner of the concourse in the early twentieth century and look northwards beneath the impressive glass and iron overall roof erected by the Butterley Company to the design of William Barlow, the Midland Railway's consulting engineer. On the right we see a Midland tank engine, which has worked in a train of empty coaching stock. (Commercial postcard / P. Laming collection)

3. Barlow's magnificent roof boasted a span of 240ft., length of 689ft and, at its apex, stood 100ft above the tracks. This view again looks north and was taken from the cab road alongside platform 5. (Commercial postcard / P. Laming collection)

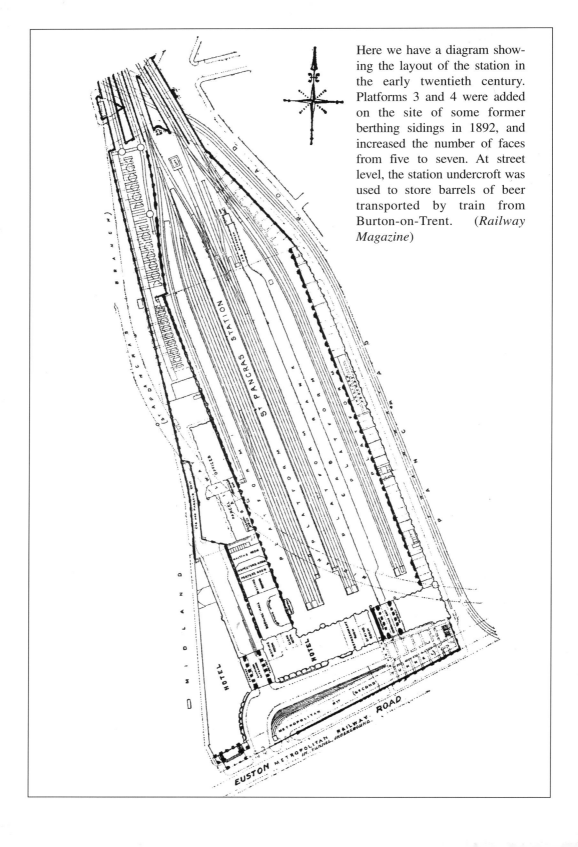

Here we have a diagram showing the layout of the station in the early twentieth century. Platforms 3 and 4 were added on the site of some former berthing sidings in 1892, and increased the number of faces from five to seven. At street level, the station undercroft was used to store barrels of beer transported by train from Burton-on-Trent. (*Railway Magazine*)

4. Compared with the architectural and engineering splendour presented by the station in general, the access stairs leading from Pancras Road were perhaps disappointing. This view dates from the 1970s and includes a large white-on-maroon enamel nameboard which had been erected around two decades earlier. (South Chingford Railway Circle)

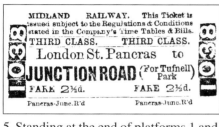

5. Standing at the end of platforms 1 and 2 around the same time, we look north and, on the left, see the signal box which replaced earlier cabins at St. Pancras Station and St. Pancras Junction on 6th October 1957 and remained in use until 6th July 1982. Further views of this station appear in the Middleton Press album *St. Pancras to St. Albans*. (South Chingford Railway Circle)

6. After losing its suburban traffic when Bedford trains were transferred to the Thameslink route in 1988, St. Pancras was used by main line trains only. During the 1990s it was decided that the station would be adapted to take services using the new Channel Tunnel Rail Link and an ambitious rebuilding scheme was subsequently set into motion. Because of its Grade I listed status, the main structure could not be substantially altered, so two new sets of platforms were planned either side of the formation, beyond the bounds of Barlow's roof. Work on these duly commenced and, once the first set had been completed, it became possible to close the original premises for modernisation. This view looks north on the last night, 9th April 2004, and shows the new Eastern Interim station, brightly illuminated behind the Midland Mainline turbo unit. (J. Downing)

7 In this view we are looking from Pancras Road towards the spacious entrance of the Eastern Interim station which opened on Easter Monday, 12th April 2004. At the time it was dealing with Midland Mainline services, but these were to be transferred to a similar addition on the western side of the formation which was then under construction. The project was expected to be completed by 2007 when the original station of 1868, with an altered platform arrangement, would be brought into use for Eurostar traffic, whilst the Eastern Interim premises would deal with domestic services to and from Kent, travelling by way of the Channel Tunnel Rail Link. (Gresley Society)

SOMERS TOWN GOODS DEPOT

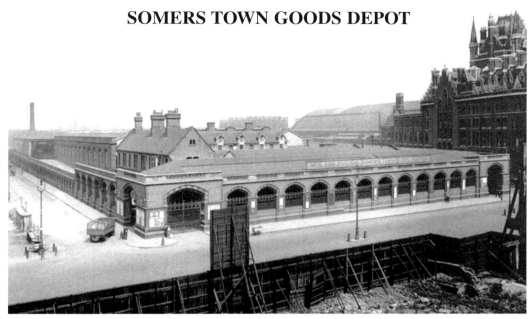

8. Opened as 'St. Pancras New Goods' on 1st November 1887 and renamed Somers Town on 1st August 1892, this depot was bounded to the east by Midland Road and west by Ossulston Street. This view was taken from behind a building site on the south side of Euston Road and shows the frontage in pre-grouping days with part of St. Pancras station on the right. The depot closed to general goods traffic on 5th June 1967, but handled coal until 23rd April 1968. In 1975 the decision was made for it to be demolished and much of the site was subsequently redeveloped for the new British Library. (British Rail)

MIDLAND AND LONDON, TILBURY, AND SOUTHEND RAILWAYS (via Tottenham and Forest Gate Railway).

WEEKDAYS.

[Timetable with numerous columns of times for stations including Bradford, Leeds, Sheffield, Liverpool (Mid. Cen.), Manchester (Mid. Cen.) (Victoria), Derby, Nottingham, Leicester, Moorgate Street dep., King's Cross (Met.), ST. PANCRAS, Camden Road, Kentish Town, Junction Road, Upper Holloway, Hornsey Road, Crouch Hill, Harringay Park (G'n Lane), St. Ann's Road, South Tottenham, Black Horse Road, Walthamstow, Leyton, Leytonstone, Wanstead Park, Woodgrange Park, East Ham arr., East Ham dep., Upton Park, Plaistow, West Ham, Bromley, Burdett Road, Stepney, Fenchurch Street, East Ham arr., Barking, Dagenham, Hornchurch, Upminster, East Horndon, Laindon, Rainham, Purfleet, Grays, Tilbury Docks, Tilbury, Gravesend, Low Street, Stanford-le-Hope, Pitsea, Benfleet, Leigh, Westcliff-on-Sea, SOUTHEND-on-SEA, Shoeburyness.]

A—Saturdays only.
B—Bank Holiday excepted.
C—These times apply during July and August only.
D—Monday mornings excepted.
F—Saturdays only, F. passengers for these Stations leave East Ham at 2.34 p.m.
G—Saturdays and Bank Holiday excepted.
H—Saturdays only. Passengers for these Stations leave East Ham at 1.57 p.m.

J—Via Barking.
K—Saturdays excepted.
L—Will not run on Saturdays in September.
N—Mondays only, Bank Holiday excepted.
P—Leaves at 2.30 p.m. on Saturdays.

R—On Mondays leaves Leeds at 3.0, Sheffield at 4.2, and Nottingham at 4.15 a.m.
S—Mondays and Saturdays only in July and August.
U—Saturdays and Bank Holiday excepted.
X—On Saturdays leave East Ham 3.49, arrive Upton Park 3.53, Plaistow 3.56, Burdett Road 4.11, Stepney 4.12, and Fenchurch Street 4.20 p.m.

† The 6.0, 7.5, and 9.50 a.m. St. Pancras to Tilbury are run in conjunction with the New Palace Steamers, Ltd., and are liable to be cancelled on any day when the boats do not run through unforeseen circumstances.

Where a thin line appears between the hour and minute figures it indicates "p.m."

Public timetable of 1902 (K. Romig collection)

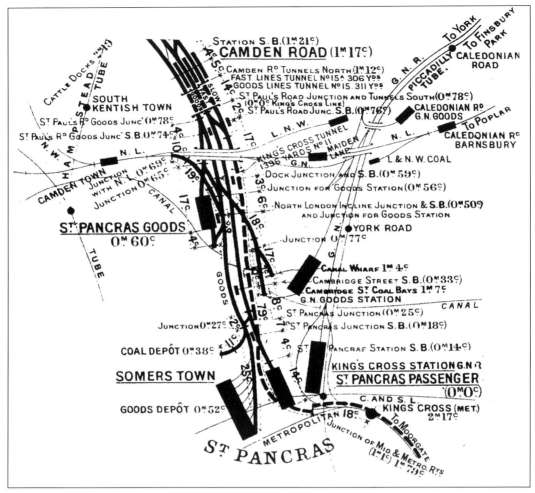

Before continuing northwards towards Kentish Town and the junctions with the Tottenham & Hampstead line, let us look at this map which is taken from the Midland Railway Distance Diagrams of 1914. The complex of lines within the area is apparent and, at first glance, perhaps confusing. However, as the original was produced for the use of Midland employees, the company's lines are shown bolder than the others, so the route is easy to follow. In the days of mechanical signalling, a layout such as this, with lots of pointwork and numerous junctions, required a number of individual signal boxes and those belonging to the Midland are all included. We will now look at some of these boxes and their immediate surroundings.

9. Having left St. Pancras behind, we come to Cambridge Street, which was located 33 chains from the terminus and signalled the passenger lines only. It functioned from 31st July 1892 until 6th October 1957 and the photograph dates from its final decade. The view looks south and includes the St. Pancras coal drops in the middle distance.   (Stephenson Locomotive Society)

10. Continuing a further 17 chains we reach the junction with the North London Incline, where the signal box was attached to a wall of the adjoining St. Pancras goods depot to give it extra stability. The box seen here replaced an earlier cabin on 23rd October 1892 and remained in use until 31st December 1961, when its place was taken by a ground frame. It controlled access to a steeply graded single-track link with the North London Railway, which passed above the Midland line a little to the north of the junction. (Stephenson Locomotive Society)

11. Remaining at the same location, we move a little further north and look back towards the box. Right of centre we see an 0-6-0T locomotive with a single cattle wagon standing on the North London Incline itself, whilst behind stands St. Pancras goods depot. This was partially brought into use from July 1862, but because the MR London Extension was still unfinished, traffic had to be routed by way of a connection off the Great Northern Railway. Goods trains travelling over the new Midland line reached the depot in September 1867 and the premises became fully functional on 9th March 1868. Just over a century later, the depot succumbed to road competition and it closed on 29th April 1968. (Stephenson Locomotive Society)

12. 59 chains from the terminus stood the box at Dock Junction which replaced an earlier cabin on 31st July 1892. This view was taken in the 1950s when the building was nearing the end of its days. (Stephenson Locomotive Society)

13. A new signal box at Dock Junction opened on 27th May 1956 to replace its 1892 predecessor which had been located 10 yards further north. It remained in use until 15th July 1979, having only signalled the Fast lines since the previous month. Our photograph, dating from 1975, looks north and includes the bridge which carries the North London Line over the Midland. (A. Vaughan collection)

14. We move on to St. Pauls Road Passenger Junction box, which had been resited twice since opening in 1868. The cabin shown here was the last to carry the name and stood 76 chains from St. Pancras. It opened on 18th September 1898 and closed from 7th October 1956, having been provided with a new lever frame in September 1919. A view of St. Pauls Road Goods Junction box, which was located 2 chains closer to the terminus appears in the Middleton Press album *St. Pancras to St. Albans*. Officially the junctions were referred to as being at *St.* Paul's Road, but as can be seen, this did not appear on the nameboard. (D. Lawrence)

CAMDEN ROAD

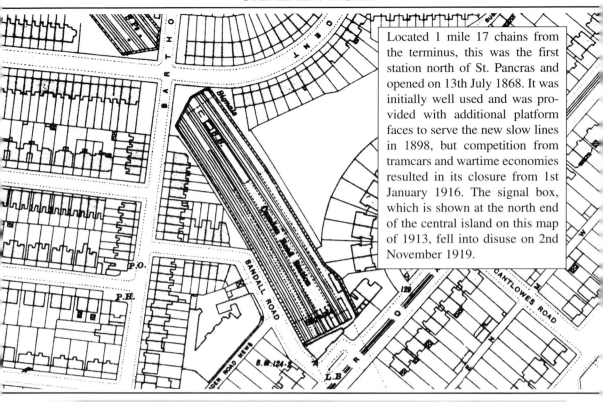

Located 1 mile 17 chains from the terminus, this was the first station north of St. Pancras and opened on 13th July 1868. It was initially well used and was provided with additional platform faces to serve the new slow lines in 1898, but competition from tramcars and wartime economies resulted in its closure from 1st January 1916. The signal box, which is shown at the north end of the central island on this map of 1913, fell into disuse on 2nd November 1919.

15. After closure the platform awnings were removed, but the platforms themselves, along with the former street level building, continued to stand. Here we see the latter as it appeared around the mid-1960s, having been converted into a filling station. (D. Jones collection)

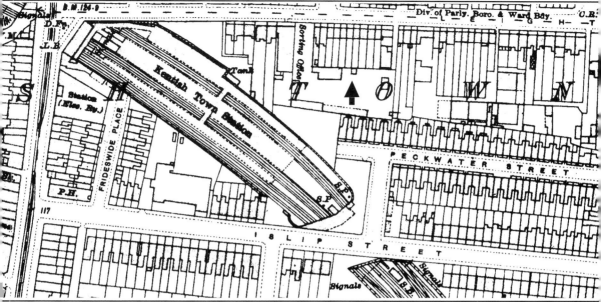

The station opened on 13th July 1868 and can be seen on this map of 1913. It originally comprised two platform faces, but the number was increased to four in 1898 when new Slow lines were added. The adjoining tube station was opened by the Charing Cross, Euston & Hampstead Railway on 22nd June 1907 and now forms part of London Underground's Northern Line.

16. Eight chains south-east of the station stood Islip Street Junction signal box, which is shown towards the bottom of the map reproduced above. This view looks north-west and shows the cabin as it appeared in BR days. It was demolished following an accident on 23rd December 1966 and not reinstated. (Stephenson Locomotive Society)

17.   This view from the early 1900s looks north along Kentish Town Road and shows part of the station's street level building on the extreme right, with a horse-drawn omnibus picking up passengers outside. This building became redundant on 7th June 1981, when a new footbridge linking its platforms with the adjoining tube station resulted in all tickets being issued from the London Transport booking office. (Charles Martin Series postcard / D. Jones collection)

18.   Standing at the London end of platform 4, we look north-west towards the footbridge. The fashions displayed by the lady on the left suggests that the photograph was taken in the late 1920s or early 1930s. (P. Laming collection)

19. Moving on to 23rd August 1947, we see Stanier Class 3MT 2-6-2T No. 114 which has just arrived at Platform 1 with the 12.25pm train from Barking. The skeletal ironwork of the canopy on the left typifies the partial dereliction displayed by many London area stations during the post-World War II period. (H.C. Casserley)

20. Trains to and from Barking last served Kentish Town on Saturday 3rd January 1981. The morning was bright and sunny, but unfortunately winter sunshine often results in deep, contrasty shadows as seen here. The diesel multiple unit has worked in from the Tottenham & Hampstead route and, having crossed from the up to the down line, awaits departure from Platform 2. (I. Baker).

21.   Station alterations, which included the closure of the original street level building, resulted in Platform 4 being temporarily closed from 5th July 1982 until 3rd February 1983, when Platform 3 was permanently taken out of commission. Here we are standing on the 1981 footbridge, looking towards St. Pancras and can see the disused, overgrown Platform 3 in the centre. (B.P. Pask)

22. To the right of this view from the early twentieth century we see the entrance to the Coal and Cattle depot at Kentish Town, which lay west of the passenger station and functioned until 2nd August 1971. For many years the adjoining coal office boasted a window display which featured attractive models of a locomotive and wagons. (Commercial postcard / D. Jones collection)

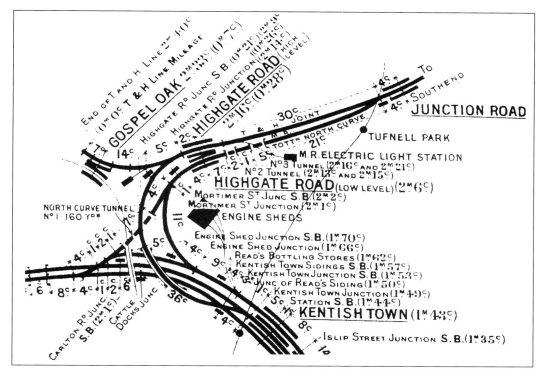

This Midland Railway Distance Diagram of 1914 shows the links with the Tottenham & Hampstead route to the north-west of Kentish Town station. The initial connection opened to goods traffic on 3rd January 1870 and passengers six months later on 1st July. It was known as the Tottenham South Curve or 'Highgate Incline' and diverged from the down side at Kentish Town Junction. It climbed at a gradient of 1 in 48 and is shown on the left, crossing above the main line. The Tottenham North Curve linked the junctions at Carlton Road and Junction Road and opened for freight traffic in the early months of 1883. This allowed through running between the industrial Midlands and the London Docks and was located partly in tunnel. In December 1900, a third connection was added when the Kentish Town Curve was opened between Engine Shed Junction and Mortimer Street Junction. This served a new low level station at Highgate Road and was less taxing for locomotives than the steeply graded Tottenham South Curve of 1870.

23.   We start our exploration of connections to the north-west of Kentish Town, with this view of LMSR Class 4F 0-6-0 No. 4590 which has just cleared the bridge over the main line and is beginning its descent of the 1 in 48 Tottenham South Curve with an up freight working on 30th June 1945. Down trains using this link onto the THJR often required a banking engine which would provide assistance from St. Pancras goods depot to Highgate Road. (H.C. Casserley)

24.   Here we see Engine Shed Junction as it appeared in September 1975, with the main line heading north-west and the 1900 Kentish Town Curve diverging to the right. The bridge carrying the Tottenham South Curve is seen on the left, with Carlton Road Junction signal box just visible through one of the arches. Engine Shed Junction cabin, located 1 mile 70 chains from St Pancras, was opened on 16th April 1899, altered the following year for the opening of the curve, and closed from 6th December 1981.   (A. Vaughan)

25. On the main line, immediately west of the Tottenham South Curve bridge stood Cattle Dock Junction signal box, which controlled access to an array of sidings. In this view we see BR Standard Class 4MT 2-6-0 No. 76039 leaving the yard with a down freight in July 1964. The box had opened on 23rd May 1936 to replace an earlier cabin called Cattle Docks Junction, which dated from March 1903, and remained in use until 24th October 1964. (G. Silcock)

26. Continuing beyond the Tottenham South Curve bridge we reach the junction at Carlton Road and see the St. Pancras and City slow lines to our right and the 1883 link with the Tottenham & Hampstead route diverging into the North Curve Tunnel No. 1 on the left. This eastward view was taken in May 1978 and includes the signal box which replaced an earlier cabin in October 1964 and closed on 22nd October 1978. (P.E.B. Butler)

27.   From the window of the 12.26pm train from Kentish Town to Southend on 25th May 1960, we look north and see Class 4F 0-6-0 No. 44532 as she approaches the signal box at Mortimer Street Junction. The embankment on the left carries the Tottenham South Curve, whilst the buildings to the right are part of the Kentish Town locomotive depot. (H.C. Casserley)

28.   The box at Mortimer Street Junction included some unusual point rodding and signal wiring, which is seen here on 12th May 1978. The first cabin at this location opened on 2nd April 1883, but closed on 12th August 1900 when a new box serving the junction with the Kentish Town Curve was brought into use. This second cabin, located 2 miles 2 chains from St. Pancras, was abolished on 22nd October 1978, but the Kentish Town Curve remained in use and continued to be served by passenger trains until January 1981. (P.E.B. Butler)

GOSPEL OAK

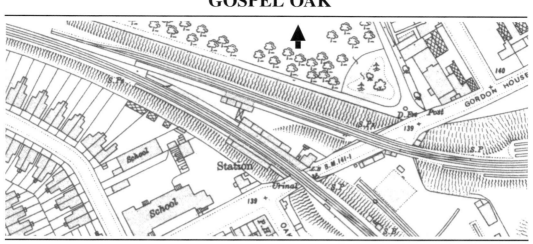

Before continuing with our exploration of the lines east of Mortimer Street Junction, we will briefly deviate westwards and take a look at Gospel Oak. This Ordnance Survey map shows the premises as they appeared in 1912, with the Hampstead Junction line station below and the single THJR platform above. The Hampstead Junction station opened as Kentish Town on 2nd January 1860, but was renamed Gospel Oak seven years later. The Tottenham & Hampstead platform was brought into use on 4th June 1888 and was used as a terminus, because the junction with the HJR had not been laid. The two routes were eventually joined on 23rd January 1916, but the connection was intended for wartime traffic only and was subsequently severed on 3rd September 1922. The junction was reinstated on 5th November 1939 soon after the outbreak of World War II and was brought into regular traffic use on 11th March 1940.

29. This undated view from LMSR days looks eastwards and shows the up North London Line platform in the foreground with the THJR station behind. As can be seen, this had its own building, although it appears to have been rarely photographed. It officially remained open until September 1926, but was retained for occasional use, generally Bank Holiday Mondays, until the final train departed on 7th August 1939. (D. Hanson collection)

30. On Sunday 27th April 1958, a special train organised by the Railway Correspondence & Travel Society called at the old THJR station and many passengers alighted to explore the overgrown platform. The locomotive, Class N7/4 0-6-2T No. 69614, made an attractive picture, but unfortunately, by this time, the old station building had long since been demolished. (J. Langford)

31. The tracks were later re-aligned and a new bay platform was constructed at a slightly higher level than the adjoining North London Line station. This became the terminus of the Barking service after 5th January 1981 and is seen here on 13th December 1980 before the work had been completed. The signal box was destroyed by fire in the small hours of 11th March 1985 and subsequently replaced. (Stephenson Locomotive Society)

32. In addition to the bay road, the formation on the former THJR side at Gospel Oak includes a pair of tracks which are used by through freight trains. This view looks east in the 1980s and includes part of the up North London Line building behind the shelter on the right. (B.P. Pask)

33. Moving on to the Spring of 2005, we see passengers joining unit No.150130 shortly before it departs for Barking. To the left of the camera is the pathway which links the bay with the up North London Line platform. The replacement signal box stands behind the rear coach. (I. Baker)

In addition to Bank Holiday traffic, it seems that the former THJR station was also used by trains serving sporting events after its official closure. The existence of this LNER ticket, which was issued on 22nd October 1932, indicates that a series of football specials were operated between Gospel Oak and Northumberland Park, possibly in connection with home games played by Tottenham Hotspur Football Club. (B.P. Pask)

CHEAP RETURN TICKETS

ISSUED DAILY UNTIL FURTHER NOTICE FROM STATIONS BETWEEN

ST. PANCRAS & WOODGRANGE PARK
TO
SOUTHEND-ON-SEA.

RETURN FARE:

First Class, 5s. 2/6 First Class, 5s.

The tickets will be available at Leigh and Westcliff-on-Sea.

(For times of departure and return see small handbills.)

NOTE.—Passengers leaving the trains at intermediate stations other than Leigh and Westcliff-on-Sea will forfeit their excursion tickets, and be required to pay the full ordinary fare.

Children under 3 years of age, free ; above 3 and under 12, half-fares.

No luggage allowed.

The tickets are not transferable, and are available to return on day of issue only.

WEEK-END TICKETS are issued every FRIDAY and SATURDAY
AS FOLLOWS, TO
SOUTHEND-ON-SEA AND SHOEBURYNESS
BY ANY TRAIN.

FARES THERE AND BACK.

Stations.	SOUTHEND-ON-SEA. Week-end.		SHOEBURYNESS. Week-end.	
	1st class.	3rd class.	1st class.	3rd class.
ST. PANCRAS .... Camden Town .... Kentish Town .... Highgate Road .... Junction Road .... Upper Holloway .... Hornsey Road .... Crouch Hill .... Harringay Park, Green Lanes.. St. Ann's Road............. South Tottenham .... Black Horse Road.......... Walthamstow .... Leyton .... Leytonstone .... WANSTEAD PARK............	6/0	3/6	6/8	3/10

Children under 3 years of age, free ; above 3 and under 12, half-fares. The tickets are not transferable, and are only available to the station for which they are issued, with the two exceptions given below. If used to any other station, the passenger will have to pay the difference between the amount paid for the week-end ticket and the fare to such station, and the return half of the ticket will also be forfeited.

RETURN JOURNEY.—The tickets are available for return by any train on the day of issue, or on any day up to and including the following Tuesday.

The tickets will be available for alighting at Leigh and Westcliff-on-Sea.

All information with regard to these tickets, also for the conveyance of school and other parties to Southend-on-Sea, may be obtained of Mr. Snow, St. Pancras Station, N.W., at the stations, or from the Assistant-Manager, London, Tilbury and Southend Railway, Fenchurch Street Terminus, London, E.C.

For further particulars see special bills.

K. Romig collection

HIGHGATE ROAD JUNCTION

34. Highgate Road Junction was where the MR's Tottenham South Curve joined the THJR line, 14 chains east of Gospel Oak. Since opening there had been three signal boxes serving this location and it is the third, opened around 1920, which we see here. The photograph was taken on 12th May 1965 and includes the stairway which had clearly been modified in later years. The box stood within the 'vee' of the junction and remained in use until 5th September 1965. (N.D. Mundy)

WILLESDEN, GOSPEL OAK, WALTHAMSTOW, STRATFORD, and CHINGFORD.—Great Eastern.

Miles.	Fares from Highgate Road. Single. 1 cl. s. d.	2 cl. s. d.	3 cl. s. d.	Return. 1 cl. s. d.	2 cl. s. d.	3 cl. s. d.	Week Days.	mrn	mrn	mrn	mrn	mrn	mrn	mrn	mrn	aft	aft	aft	aft	aft	aft	aft	aft	aft	aft	aft
							Willesden Junction dep.	....	7 52	....	9 2	....	9 37	1037	1152	1252	1 37	2 37	3 37	4 52	5 37	6 37	7 37	8 37	9 37	1027
							Gospel Oak arr.	....	8 3	....	9 15	....	9 53	1053	12 8	1 8	1 53	2 53	3 53	5 8	5 53	6 53	7 53	8 53	9 53	1053
—							Gospel Oak dep.	6 55	8 23	8 47	9 26	9 40	1010	11 8	1212	1 16	2 4	3 5	4 8	5 15	6 2	7 6	8 5	9 5	1010	11 0
¼							Highgate Road	6 57	8 25	8 49	9 28	9 42	1012	1110	1214	1 18	2 6	3 7	4 10	5 17	6 4	7 8	8 7	9 7	1012	11 2
¾	0 3	0 2	0 1	0 6	0 4	0 2	Junction Road ‡	6 59	8 27	8 51	9 30	9 44	1014	1112	1216	1 20	2 8	3 9	4 12	5 19	6 6	7 10	8 9	9 9	1014	11 4
1¼	0 3	0 2	0 1	0 6	0 4	0 2	Upper Holloway	7 1	8 29	8 53	9 32	9 46	1016	1114	1218	1 22	2 10	3 11	4 14	5 21	6 8	7 12	8 11	9 11	1016	11 6
1½	0 3	0 2½	0 1	0 6	0 4	0 2	Hornsey Road §	7 3	8 31	8 55	9 34	9 48	1018	1116	1220	1 24	2 12	3 13	4 16	5 23	6 10	7 14	8 13	9 13	1018	11 8
2	0 3	0 2½	0 1½	0 6	0 5	0 3	Crouch Hill	7 5	8 33	8 57	9 36	9 50	1020	1118	1222	1 26	2 14	3 15	4 18	5 25	6 12	7 16	8 15	9 15	1020	1110
2¾	0 5	0 4	0 2½	0 9	0 7	0 5	Harringay Park	7 8	8 36	9 0	9 39	9 53	1023	1121	1225	1 29	2 17	3 18	4 21	....	6 15	7 19	8 18	9 18	1023	1113
3¼	0 6	0 4½	0 3	0 10	0 8	0 6	St. Ann's Road	7 10	8 38	9 2	9 41	9 55	1025	1123	1227	1 31	2 19	3 20	4 23	....	6 17	7 21	8 20	9 20	1025	1115
4	0 7	0 5	0 3½	0 11	0 9	0 6	South Tottenham	7 12	8 40	9 4	9 43	9 57	1027	1125	1229	1 33	2 21	3 22	4 25	5 29	6 19	7 23	8 22	9 22	1027	1117
6½	0 10	0 7	0 4½	1 3	0 10	0 7	St. James's Street *	....	8 47	....	9 48	....	1033	1131	1235	1 39	2 29	3 29	4 31	5 41	6 25	7 29	8 28	9 28	1033	1123
7¾	0 9	0 6	0 4	1 1	0 9	0 7	Lea Bridge	7 17	8 28	....	....	10 2	1130	....	....	1 47	3 22	4 24	5 27	5 52	7 21	....	8 52	9 59	11 8	....
10	0 9	0 6	0 4	1 1	0 9	0 7	Stratford ‖ arr.	7 30	8 33	9 19	....	....	1138	....	....	1 55	3 30	4 32	5 37	6 3	7 31	....	9 2	10 7	1114	....
6¾	0 10	0 7	0 5½	1 3	0 10	0 8	Hoe Street *	Mons only.	8 50	Thro' to S'thend	9 51	....	1036	1134	1238	1 42	2 32	3 32	4 34	5 44	6 28	7 32	8 31	9 31	1036	1126
7¾	1 1	0 9	0 5½	1 7	1 1	0 8	Wood Street *		8 52		9 53	....	1039	1137	1240	1 44	2 34	3 34	4 36	5 46	6 31	7 34	8 33	9 33	1038	1128
9	1 4	0 11	0 7	1 11	1 4	0 11	Highams Park †		8 58		9 59	....	1044	1142	1246	1 50	2 40	3 40	4 42	5 52	6 37	7 40	8 39	9 39	1044	1130
11	1 6	1 0	0 9	2 3	1 4	0 6	Chingford arr.		9 3		10 4	....	1049	1147	1251	1 55	2 45	3 45	4 47	5 57	6 42	7 45	8 44	9 44	1050	1144

Mls	Fares. 1 cl.	2 cl.	3 cl.	Return. 2 cl.	2 cl.	3 cl.	Week Days.	mrn	mrn	mrn	mrn	mrn	aft	aft	aft	aft	aft	aft	aft	aft	aft	aft	aft	aft	aft	aft
—							Chingford dep.	7 39	8 23	9 16	1020	11 2	1210	1 20	2 20	3 20	aft to Ilford 3 35 aft	4 18	5 5	6 20	7 20	8 8	S'thend Thro fm	Mons only.	9 7	1015
2	0 3	0 2	0 1	0 4	0 3	0 2	Highams Park †	7 43	8 27	9 21	1024	11 6	1220	1 24	2 24	3 24		4 22	5 9	6 24	7 24	8 12			9 12	1019
3¼	0 6	0 4	0 3	0 9	0 6	0 4	Wood Street *	7 47	8 31	9 26	1028	1110	1224	1 28	2 28	3 28		4 26	5 13	6 28	7 28	8 16			9 17	1023
4¼	0 9	0 6	0 4	1 1	0 9	0 6	Hoe Street *	7 50	8 34	9 29	1031	1113	1227	1 31	2 31	3 31		4 29	5 16	6 31	7 31	8 19			9 20	1026
—	1 4	1 0	0 6	2 0	1 4	1 0	Stratford ‖ dep.	7 28	....	8 31	....	1040	1152	1250	2b12	2c35		3 31	4 57	....	6 24	7 59	8 34	9 10	9 5	1010
—	1 0	0 9	0 6	1 6	1 2	0 9	Lea Bridge	7 33	....	8 36	....	1045	1157	1255	2b17	2c40	a	3 36	5 2	....	6 29	8 4	8 43	9 15	9 10	1015
4½	0 10	0 7	0 4½	1 3	0 10	0 7	St. James's Street *	7 52	8 36	9 31	1033	1115	1229	1 33	2 34	3 33	....	4 31	5 18	6 33	7 33	8 21	....	....	9 22	1028
7	1 0	0 8	0 6	1 4	1 0	0 8	South Tottenham	7 58	8 44	9 37	1040	1121	1235	1 39	2 41	3 39	a	4 37	5 24	6 40	7 39	8 28	8 49	9 20	9 29	1034
7½	1 0	0 8	0 6	1 6	1 0	0 9	St. Ann's Road	8 0	8 46	9 39	1042	1123	1237	1 41	2 43	3 41	a	4 39	5 26	6 42	7 41	8 30	8 51	9 22	9 31	1036
8½	1 2	0 9	0 7	1 9	1 1	0 10	Harringay Park	8 2	8 48	9 41	1044	1125	1239	1 43	2 45	3 43	a	4 41	5 28	6 44	7 43	8 32	8 53	9 24	9 33	1038
9	1 3	0 10	0 8	1 10	1 2	0 10	Crouch Hill	8 5	8 51	9 44	1047	1128	1242	1 46	2 48	3 46	a	4 44	5 31	6 47	7 46	8 35	8 56	9 27	9 36	1041
9½	1 4	0 10	0 8	2 0	1 2	0 10	Hornsey Road §	8 7	8 53	9 46	1049	1130	1244	1 48	2 50	3 48	a	4 46	5 33	6 49	7 48	8 37	8 58	9 29	9 38	1043
9¾	1 5	0 11	0 8	2 2	1 3	0 11	Upper Holloway	8 9	8 55	9 48	1051	1132	1246	1 50	2 52	3 50	a	4 48	5 35	6 51	7 50	8 39	9 0	9 31	9 40	1045
10¼	1 6	1 0	0 9	2 3	1 4	1 0	Junction Road ‡	8 11	8 57	9 50	1053	1134	1248	1 52	2 54	3 52	a	4 50	5 37	6 53	7 52	8 41	9 2	9 33	9 42	1047
10½	1 6	1 0	0 9	2 3	1 4	1 0	Highgate Road	8 13	8 59	9 52	1055	1136	1250	1 54	2 56	3 54	a	4 52	5 39	6 55	7 54	8 43	9 4	9 35	9 44	1049
11	1 6	1 0	0 9	2 3	1 4	1 0	Gospel Oak arr.	8 15	9 1	9 54	1057	1138	1252	1 56	2 58	3 56	a	4 54	5 41	6 57	7 56	8 45	9 7	9 37	9 46	1051
—	....	....	....	....	....	....	Gospel Oak dep.	8 29	9 14	9 59	1114	1144	1259	1 59	3 14	3 59	....	4 59	5 46	7 14	8 14	8 59	9 14	....	9 59	1059
16	....	....	....	....	....	....	Willesden Jun. 310 arr.	8 46	9 30	1016	1130	12 0	1 16	2 16	3 30	4 16	....	5 16	6 2	7 30	8 30	9 16	9 30	....	1016	1116

a Stops to set down. b Saturdays only. c Except Saturdays. * Walthamstow. † Highams Park and Hale End. ‡ Station for Tufnell Park; § for Hornsey Rise. ‖ Stratford (West Ham). For Stations between Willesden and Gospel Oak, see pages 302 to 304.

July 1899

HIGHGATE ROAD

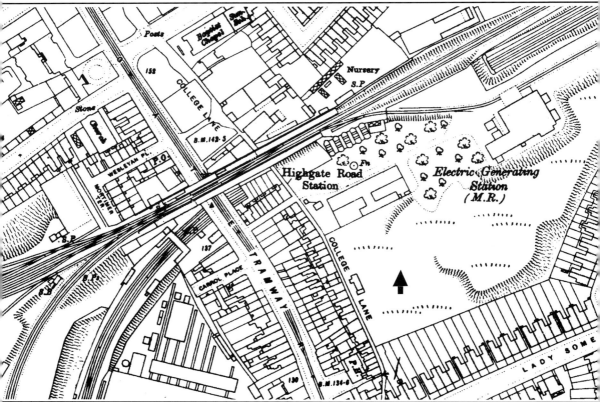

This Ordnance Survey map shows the complex of lines around Highgate Road in 1912. The platforms indicated on the upper line are those of the original station which opened on 21st July 1868 and served as a terminus for THJR trains until the short extension to Gospel Oak was opened twenty years later. Below these, on the left we see the low level platforms which were opened on 17th December 1900 to serve the newly constructed Kentish Town Curve. Further left lies the Tottenham South Curve and the formation towards Gospel Oak, with Highgate Road Junction box standing between the diverging routes. On the right is the Midland Railway electric generating station, which supplied current for station lighting and the suchlike and, above this, the tracks from Kentish Town and Carlton Road Junction emerge from the North Curve No. 2 Tunnel. Although served by a common entrance, the two stations at Highgate Road are best regarded as separate entities, as the High Level belonged to the THJR, whilst the Low Level was purely Midland. Both suffered as a result of tramway competition and were closed from 1st October 1915 and 1st March 1918 respectively, with the latter being comparatively short-lived. The original station was renamed Highgate Road for Parliament Hill in November 1894 and although the suffix subsequently applied to both sets of platforms, it was officially dropped from 1st July 1903.

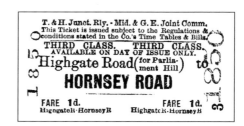

35. Highgate Road High Level station, located 2 miles 16 chains from St. Pancras by way of the Tottenham South Curve, was demolished in 1919 and no photographs of its buildings are known. They were built of brick and resembled those at Upper Holloway and Crouch Hill, as did the platform canopies, but unless a photograph eventually surfaces this cannot be confirmed. The view reproduced here shows ex-WD 2-8-0 No. 63173 receiving attention from a member of her crew as she stands at the station site in the late 1940s. To the left we see some meagre remains of the erstwhile eastbound platform and the wall which backed it, but sadly, little else. (Gresley Society)

36. The street level entrance was located beneath the bridge on the west side of Highgate Road and has long since been converted for non-railway purposes. This view, taken in 1981 includes the remains of the former lamp bracket above the doorway, although this subsequently disappeared. (J.E. Connor)

37. When platforms were opened on the new Kentish Town Curve, 2 miles 6 chains from St Pancras, in 1900, they were dubbed as Highgate Road Low Level whilst the original premises became known as 'High Level'. From the various specimens seen by the author, this differential does not seem to have appeared on tickets, although of course there may have been exceptions. After closure in 1915, the High Level station was still used by passengers as a means of accessing the Low Level platforms, but this arrangement ceased when Highgate Road fell into complete disuse three years later. Again little is known of the Low Level station's appearance, although the positioning of its buildings may be gleaned from Ordnance Survey maps of the period. Some platform remains are known to have survived along with the covered footbridge which linked them until the 1930s, but these were eventually swept away. This view shows a diesel multiple unit passing the site in December 1980 as it nears the end of its journey from Barking to Kentish Town. Behind it the new brickwork above the arches may indicate where the wall had been 'made good' after the High Level station was demolished, or perhaps it was just the result of a subsequent repair. (D. Pearson)

JUNCTION ROAD JUNCTION

38.   Junction Road Junction was where the lines from Kentish Town and Carlton Road joined the route serving Gospel Oak. This westward view, which dates from the 1970s, shows the ex-MR tracks diverging through the left hand arch, whilst the former THJR continues to the right. The signal box, which stood 2 miles 42 chains from St. Pancras, replaced an earlier cabin around April 1883 and, although it had undergone a minor re-siting in October 1912, it remained in use until 10th November 1985, when its duties passed to a two-level Portakabin at Upper Holloway. After closure the box was vandalised and it was demolished following fire damage. (R.L. Plassard)

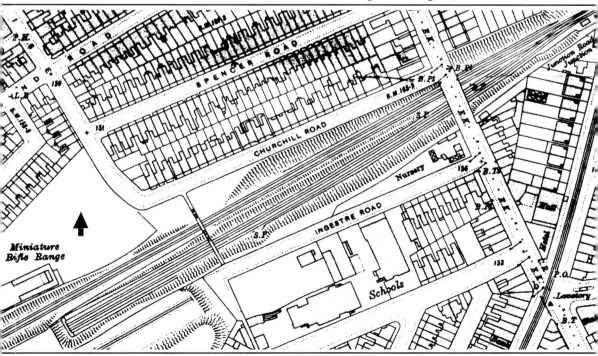

The map of 1912 shows the signal box at top right, with the two diverging lines continuing westward. The southernmost tracks are those serving the Kentish Town and Carlton Road routes, and these can be seen disappearing into the North Curve Tunnel No. 2 near the bottom left.

JUNCTION ROAD

4 chains to the north east of Junction Road Junction box stood the passenger station at Junction Road suffixed 'for Tufnell Park'. This opened on 1st January 1872 and comprised two platforms, accessed from the street level booking office by means of a footbridge and stairs. The map of 1912 shows the station to the left, along with the expanse of sidings which stretch almost to Upper Holloway. On the up side we see the GER Tufnell Park goods and cattle depot which opened in 1886 and remained in use until 6th May 1968. Junction Road not only suffered from tramway competition in the early twentieth century, but also the Charing Cross, Euston & Hampstead tube line which had a nearby station at Tufnell Park. At its zenith in 1902, a total of 143,447 passengers were booked at the station, but in 1922 this had dropped to just 30,251. A 1937 poem by John (later Sir John) Betjeman described the premises as "lonely" with a single gaslight to illuminate the booking hall. Closure came on 3rd May 1943 and the station was largely demolished in the following decade. Holloway Tram Depot appears in *Hampstead & Highgate Tramways* (Middleton Press).

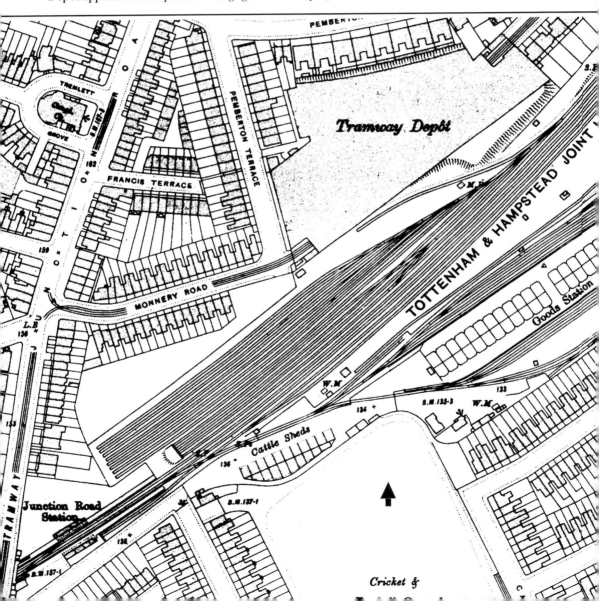

39. The wooden platform buildings are known to have still been standing in 1951, but they had gone a few years later when this somewhat murky, but atmospheric photograph was taken. We are standing on the down side, looking west and can see that part of the up platform had already been demolished. The bridge carrying Junction Road itself crosses over the tracks in the middle distance and, although far from clear, it appears that the up side stairway had not yet been removed. (D. Jones collection)

40. Looking east from the Junction Road bridge in the 1970s, we can see that the station had seemingly disappeared completely, as had the former GER goods depot, although some associated trackwork remained as sidings. To the left stands an oil terminal which occupies the site of the twelve sidings shown on the map.   (R.L. Plassard)

UPPER HOLLOWAY

Situated in cutting, Upper Holloway station was 3 miles from St. Pancras. It is seen here on the Ordnance Survey map of 1912, along with the north-eastern continuation of Tufnell Park goods depot which we have already encountered at Junction Road. Upper Holloway opened with the Tottenham - Highgate Road section of line on 21st July 1868 and was closed from 31st January 1870 until 1st October 1870, when services were temporarily suspended. According to public timetables, the station became known as Upper Holloway for St. John's Park & Highgate Hill from 1st March 1871 and Upper Holloway for St. John's Park on 1st April 1875. The suffix was officially dropped altogether from 1st July 1903, although it was still shown in the Midland Railway distance diagrams produced in 1914.

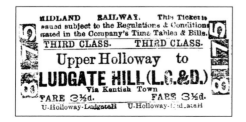

41.   It seems that the station remained little altered for many years, although the 1930s saw the addition of LMSR 'hawkseye' style nameboards as seen on the left. In this view, which was taken on 8th November 1958, we observe Stanier 2-6-2T No. 40111 running bunker-first with the 2.05pm train from Barking to Kentish Town.   (H.C. Casserley)

42.   Moving into the 1960s, it is apparent that the station still exhibited its original features and continued to do so until the second half of the decade. We are standing on the up platform, looking northeast and view a diesel multiple unit arriving on its journey from Barking to Kentish Town. (K. Romig)

43.   Upper Holloway signal box stood eight chains west of the station and replaced an earlier cabin on 5th March 1893. It was located on the down side and is seen in this view which was taken on 12th April 1985.   (D. Pearson)

44.   On 10th November 1985, both Upper Holloway and Junction Road Junction cabins were closed and their place taken by a new two-tier Portakabin signal box which is seen on the left. This photograph was taken six months before the changeover took place and includes the earlier box to the right, which was still in use at the time. The loop line on the south side was still available in 2005.   (South Chingford Railway Circle)

45. This is the street level building, as it appeared in May 1985. It subsequently fell into semi-dereliction, but was repaired and, although sporting an altered frontage, remained standing in 2005. (South Chingford Railway Circle)

46. Here we have another view of the building, but this time viewed from the station footbridge later in the same decade. By this time it was no longer serving its intended purpose as tickets were being issued on the trains by conductor-guards. (B.P. Pask)

47. Rolling stock problems in the late 1990s resulted in the brief appearance on the line of a former Southern Region 3-TC set powered by a Class 33 diesel locomotive. This view was taken from the station footbridge on 24th August 1999 and shows an eastbound working arriving at Upper Holloway with the loco propelling from the rear. The original platform buildings were demolished when the station was rationalised in the second half of the 1960s and various alterations have taken place since, including the provision of sloping walkways to improve accessibility from street level. (M. Batten)

Sundays.

	mrn	mrn	mrn	aft	aft	aft	aft	aft	aft	aft	aft	aft	aft	aft
Willesden Jun.dep.	8 55		9 55		1 13	2 30	3	1 4	1 5	1 6	1 7	1 8	1 9	1 10 10
Gospel Oak....arr.	8 51		10 11		1 28	2 47	3 17	4 17	5 17	6 17	7 17	8 17	9 17	10 26
Gospel Oak......dep.	8 54	8 53	10 36	12 49	1 49	2 49	3 49	4 49	5 49	6 49	7 49	8 49	9 35	10 35
Highgate Road......	8 56	9 0	10 38	12 51	1 51	2 51	3 51	4 51	5 51	6 51	7 51	8 51	9 37	10 37
Junction Road ‡.....	8 58	9 2	10 40	12 53	1 53	2 53	3 53	4 53	5 53	6 53	7 53	8 53	9 39	10 39
Upper Holloway.....	9 0	9 4	10 42	12 55	1 55	2 55	3 55	4 55	5 55	6 55	7 55	8 55	9 41	10 41
Hornsey Road §.....	9 2	9 6	10 44	12 57	1 57	2 57	3 57	4 57	5 57	6 57	7 57	8 57	9 43	10 43
Crouch Hill	9 4	9 8	10 46	12 59	1 59	2 59	3 59	4 59	5 59	6 59	7 59	8 59	9 45	10 45
Harringay Park.....	9 7	9 11	10 49	1 2	2 2	3 2	4 2	5 2	6 2	7 2	8 2	9 2	9 48	10 48
St. Ann's Road	9 9	9 13	10 51	1 4	2 4	3 4	4 4	5 4	6 4	7 4	8 4	9 4	9 50	10 50
South Tottenham ...	9 11	9 15	10 53	1 6	2 6	3 6	4 6	5 6	6 6	7 6	8 6	9 6	9 52	10 52
St. James's Street *.	9 18		11 0	1 13	2 13	3 13	4 13	5 13	6 13	7 13	8 13	9 13	10 1	10 58
Lea Bridge.........	9 31			1 31	2 31	3 31	4 31	5 31	6 31	7 31	8 31	9 39	10 56	....
Stratford ‖.....arr.	9 36	9 37		1 36	2 36	3 36	4 36	5 36	6 36	7 36	8 36	9 39	10 42	....
Hoe Street *.........	9 20		11 1	1 16	2 16	3 16	4 16	5 16	6 16	7 16	8 16	9 16	10 4	11 1
Wood Street *.......	9 23		11 5	1 19	2 19	3 19	4 19	5 19	6 19	7 19	8 19	9 19	10 6	11 3
Highams Park †.....	9 27		11 11	1 24	2 24	3 24	4 24	5 24	6 24	7 24	8 24	9 24	10 11	....
Chingford .... arr.	9 31		11 16	1 29	2 29	3 29	4 29	5 29	6 29	7 29	8 29	9 29	10 15	....

Sundays.

	mrn	aft	aft	aft	aft	aft	aft	aft	aft	aft	aft	aft	aft
Chingford.........dep.	9 37	12 7	1 52	2 52	3 52	4 52	5 52	6 52	7 52	8 52		9 50	....
Highams Park †.....	9 41	12 11	1 56	2 56	3 56	4 56	5 56	6 56	7 56	8 56		9 54	....
Wood Street *.......	9 45	12 15	2 0	3 0	4 0	5 0	6 0	7 0	8 0	9 0		9 58	....
Hoe Street *.........	9 48	12 18	2 3	3 3	4 3	5 3	6 3	7 3	8 3	9 3		10 1	....
Stratford ‖.....dep.	8 40	....	1 40	2 40	3 40	4 40	5 40	6 40	7 40	8 40		9 52	....
Lea Bridge.........	8 45	....	1 45	2 45	3 45	4 45	5 45	6 45	7 45	8 45		9 59	....
St. James's Street *.	9 50	12 20	5 2	5 3	5 4	5 5	5 6	5 7	5 8	5 9		10 4	....
South Tottenham ...	9 56	12 26	1 11	2 11	3 11	4 11	5 11	6 11	7 11	8 11		10 11	....
St. Ann's Road	9 58	12 28	1 13	2 13	3 13	4 13	5 13	6 13	7 13	8 13		10 13	....
Harringay Park	10 0	12 30	1 15	2 15	3 15	4 15	5 15	6 15	7 15	8 15		10 15	....
Crouch Hill	10 3	12 33	1 18	2 18	3 18	4 18	5 18	6 18	7 18	8 18		10 18	....
Hornsey Road §.....	10 5	12 35	1 20	2 20	3 20	4 20	5 20	6 20	7 20	8 20		10 20	....
Upper Holloway.....	10 7	12 37	1 22	2 22	3 22	4 22	5 22	6 22	7 22	8 22		10 22	....
Junction Road ‡.....	10 9	12 39	1 24	2 24	3 24	4 24	5 24	6 24	7 24	8 24		10 24	....
Highgate Road......	10 11	12 41	1 26	2 26	3 26	4 26	5 26	6 26	7 26	8 26		10 26	....
Gospel Oak......arr.	10 13	12 45	1 28	2 28	3 28	4 28	5 28	6 28	7 28	8 28		10 28	....
Gospel Oak....dep.	10 18	....	1 34	2 34	3 34	4 34	5 34	6 34	7 34	8 34		10 34	....
Willesden Jun.arr	10 36	....	5 52	5 03	5 34	5 25	5 26	5 37	5 38	5 39		10 53	....

July 1889

53. We stand a little to the east of the platforms in 1962 and observe a Type 2 Bo-Bo diesel loco-motive, later designated 'Class 24', rumbling through the station with what is believed to be a St. Pancras - Tilbury boat train. Prior to subsequent changes, the eastern end of the platform ramps marked the boundary between London and the erstwhile county of Middlesex, so the station was officially part of the Metropolis, but the signal box was not! (G. Silcock)

KENTISH TOWN SOUTH TOTTENHAM AND BARKING

(Second class only)
WEEKDAYS

		am T	am		am	am		am T	am	am		am	am	am SZ		am	am		noon	pm S	pm
St. Pancras	dep	5 0	....	....	....	6 0	....	6 50	....	....	....	....	....	....	....	....	....	....	....	12N 8	....
Kentish Town	,,	5 5	....	....	6 8	....	6 55	7 27	7 56	....	8 27	9 0	9 36	....	10 0	11 0	....	12 0	12 Z26	1 0
Upper Holloway	,,	5 11	5 22	....	5 57	6 *14	....	7 1	7 33	8 1	....	8 33	9 6	9 42	....	10 6	11 6	....	12 6	12 32	1 6
Crouch Hill	,,	....	5 25	....	6 0	6 17	....	7 4	7 36	8 5	....	8 36	9 9	9 45	....	10 9	11 9	....	12 9	12 35	1 9
Harringay Stadium	,,	5 16	5 28	....	6 3	6 20	....	7 7	7 39	8 8	....	8 39	9 12	9 48	....	10 12	11 12	....	12 12	12 39	1 12
South Tottenham	,,	5 20	5 31	....	6 6	6 23	....	7 10	7 42	8 11	....	8 42	9 15	9 52	....	10 15	11 15	....	12 15	12 43	1 15
Black Horse Road	,,	5 23	5 34	....	6 9	6 26	....	7 13	7 45	8 14	....	8 45	9 18	9 56	....	10 18	11 18	....	12 18	12 47	1 18
Walthamstow	,,	5 26	5 37	....	6 12	6 29	....	7 16	7 48	8 17	....	8 48	9 21	9 59	....	10 21	11 21	....	12 21	12 50	1 21
Leyton Midland Road	,,	5 29	5 40	....	6 15	6 32	....	7 19	7 51	8 20	....	8 51	9 24	10 3	....	10 24	11 24	....	12 24	12 54	1 24
Leytonstone High Road	,,	5 32	5 43	....	6 18	6 35	....	7 22	7 54	8 23	....	8 54	9 27	10 6	....	10 27	11 27	....	12 27	12 57	1 27
Wanstead Park	,,	5 35	5 46	....	6 21	6 38	....	7 25	7 57	8 26	....	8 57	9 30	10 9	....	10 30	11 30	....	12 30	1 0	1 30
Woodgrange Park	,,	5 38	5 49	....	6 24	6 41	....	7 28	8 0	8 29	....	9 0	9 33	10 17	....	10 33	11 33	....	12 33	1 6	1 33
Barking	arr	5 42	5 53	....	6 28	6 45	....	7 32	8 4	8 33	....	9 4	9 37	1026	....	10 37	11 37	....	12 37	1 10	1 37

WEEKDAYS—continued

		pm S	pm		pm	pm		pm	pm		pm	pm		pm	pm		pm	pm		pm	p.m
St. Pancras	dep																				
Kentish Town	,,	1 30	2 0	....	3 0	4 0	....	4 41	5 10	....	5 24	6 0	....	6 35	7 5	....	8 0	9 0	....	10 0	11 0
Upper Holloway	,,	1 36	2 6	....	3 6	4 6	....	4 47	5 16	....	5 30	6 6	....	6 41	7 11	....	8 6	9 6	....	10 6	11 6
Crouch Hill	,,	1 39	2 9	....	3 9	4 9	....	4 50	5 19	....	5 33	6 9	....	6 44	7 14	....	8 9	9 9	....	10 9	11 9
Harringay Stadium	,,	1 42	2 12	....	3 12	4 12	....	4 53	5 22	....	5 36	6 12	....	6 47	7 17	....	8 12	9 12	....	10 12	11 12
South Tottenham	,,	1 45	2 15	....	3 15	4 15	....	4 56	5 25	....	5 39	6 15	....	6 50	7 20	....	8 15	9 15	–..	10 15	11 15
Black Horse Road	,,	1 48	2 18	....	3 18	4 18	....	4 59	5 28	....	5 42	6 18	....	6 53	7 23	....	8 18	9 18	....	10 18	11 18
Walthamstow	,,	1 51	2 21	....	3 21	4 21	....	5 2	5 31	....	5 45	6 21	....	6 56	7 26	....	8 21	9 21	....	10 21	11 21
Leyton Midland Road	,,	1 54	2 24	....	3 24	4 24	....	5 5	5 34	....	5 48	6 24	....	6 59	7 29	....	8 24	9 24	....	10 24	11 24
Leytonstone High Road	,,	1 57	2 27	....	3 27	4 27	....	5 8	5 37	....	5 51	6 27	....	7 2	7 32	....	8 27	9 27	....	10 27	11 27
Wanstead Park	,,	2 0	2 30	....	3 30	4 30	....	5 11	5 40	....	5 54	6 30	....	7 5	7 35	....	8 30	9 30	....	10 30	11 30
Woodgrange Park	,,	2 3	2 33	....	3 33	4 33	....	5 14	5 43	....	5 57	6 33	....	7 8	7 38	....	8 33	9 33	....	10 33	11 33
Barking	arr	2 7	2 37	....	3 37	4 37	....	5 18	5 47	....	6 1	6 37	....	7 12	7 42	....	8 37	9 37	....	10 37	11 37

N—Change at Kentish Town   S—Saturdays only
Z—Through steam train to Southend-on-Sea (Central)   T—Through train from St. Pancras

April 1960

54. The old platform awnings were demolished in the second half of the 1960s and replaced by small brick-built shelters. This view shows a Barking - Kentish Town service pausing at the up side in December 1980. (G. Larkbey)

55. Standing near the top of the westbound stairway on 19th August 1998, we see multiple unit No. L721 travelling towards Gospel Oak. By this time the platforms had been technically shortened by the erection of barriers towards their eastern ends. (D. Pearson)

HARRINGAY PARK JUNCTION

The curve linking the Great Northern main line with the Tottenham & Hampstead route at Harringay has a very chequered history, which began with its authorisation in 1862. Work on its construction started soon after, but diffidence on behalf of the GNR resulted in the project stalling and the curve, seen in the diagram here, remained seemingly un-used and was lifted by 1881.

Its first revival came during World War I, when its re-installation was approved by the War Office at the end of 1915. The new curve, which was on a slightly different alignment to before, was officially opened at noon on Monday 15th May 1916, although the junction with the GNR was possibly not commissioned until a few days later. It also differed from the original layout in that the track was single whereas it had previously been double. Once again however, the curve seemed to have remained un-used and the GNR severed its junction in April 1920.

The onset of World War II resulted in a re-surgence of interest as the curve was thought to have strategic possibilities, and work on its rehabilitation commenced in November 1939. The single track connection was finally brought into use on 8th January 1940 and saw regular traffic from 11th March 1940. It remained in use in 2005.

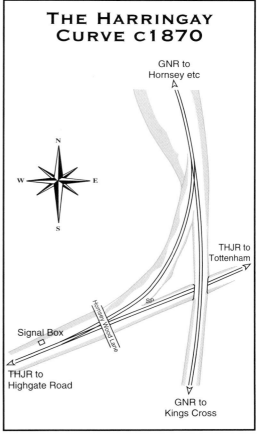

(London Railway Record)

56. Here we see ex-LMSR 4F Class 0-6-0 No. 44259 passing Harringay Park Junction signal box with an empty stock working in June 1962. (D.I.D. Loveday / Gresley Society)

57.   Although the curve has never carried a regular passenger service, it has proved useful for freight traffic and stock moves. This photograph, taken on 15th April 2002, shows Class 31 A1A-A1A No. 31 459 taking the junction with the 10.24 Hornsey - Cricklewood special train which was seemingly formed of empty electrical multiple units. A box was built to serve the junction in the late 1860s, but this was seemingly never used and was later removed. A further cabin was erected and opened on 15th May 1916, but this closed from 22nd August 1920 and was again demolished. A third box was opened on 8th January 1940 and this continued to function until being replaced by that seen here on 8th February 1959. (I. Stewart)

58.   Standing near the foot of the signal box stairs on 10th April 2001, we look east and see No. 66144 rolling past clear semaphore signals with the 09.52 Chelmsford to Mountsorrel working. Since its earliest days the Barking - Kentish Town / Gospel Oak route has proved to be a useful link for through freight services. The single track connection with the erstwhile GNR lies to the left. (I. Stewart)

HARRINGAY GREEN LANES

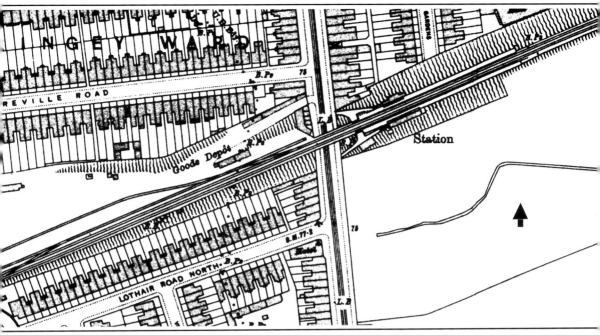

Positioned 4miles 58chains from St. Pancras, the station opened as Green Lanes on 1st June 1880 and can be seen to the right of this Ordnance Survey map which dates from 1912. It was renamed Harringay Park, Green Lanes on 30th August 1884. The suffix was eventually dropped from 18th June 1951 and a further renaming came on 27th October 1958 when the station became Harringay Stadium. The goods depot was located a little further west and is shown to the left of the map. It seems to have opened in 1882, although from the evidence of maps it is apparent that there had been a siding there since at least 1872. The yard was subject to the same name changes as the nearby passenger station, and continued to function until 3rd February 1964.

59.   From the west end of the up platform we see a Great Eastern Railway 0-4-4T approaching with a Gospel Oak - Chingford train in pre-grouping days. (J.E. Connor Collection)

60.   The station lost its original wooden platforms and buildings when it was extensively rebuilt in the 1950s. In this view, an ex-LMSR Fowler Class 3MT 2-6-2T is seen departing from the up platform whilst working between Barking and Kentish Town on 9th January 1960. To the right we see part of Harringay Stadium, which in later years was demolished for redevelopment. (T. Wright)

61. We look west on 10th September 1963 and see, to the extreme left, an additional stairway which was provided to deal with crowds attending greyhound races at the adjoining stadium. Harringay was once a popular destination for sporting enthusiasts as it also boasted an arena where boxing matches were held. (Stations UK)

62. Diesel multiple unit No. L704, carrying a Network SouthEast logo beneath its central front window, stands at the eastbound platform on 27th March 1989. (M. Batten)

63. The ticket office was accommodated in a building adjoining the westbound side and is seen here as viewed from platform level in May 1985. Propped against the fence to the right lies a blue Eastern Region name sign which had previously hung above the entrance. The building was still standing at the beginning of 2005 although it had long since ceased to be used for its original purpose and had been converted into a cafe. (South Chingford Railway Circle)

64. On 14th May 1990, the station was renamed Harringay East and is seen here sporting its new nameboards soon after. By this time the westbound building had been demolished and its counterpart on the opposite platform was boarded-up. (B.P. Pask)

65. The station was not known as Harringay East for very long, as it was renamed Harringay Green Lanes on 8th July 1991. This view looks towards Barking and was taken in March 1993. (C.D.J. Connor)

66.   The surviving 1950s building was eventually swept away and new platform shelters were erected. Subsidence problems resulted in the need to renew the platforms, which were rebuilt and shortened at their eastern end between 1999 and the beginning of 2003. The rebuilt station is seen here in January 2005 as a Silverlink Metro Class 150 diesel multiple unit departs for Gospel Oak. The platform shelters display perforated end panels, which have been installed along the route instead of glass because of constant vandalism. The subway which once linked the platforms is no longer in use as both sides now have dedicated entrances from street level and, of recent years, sloping walkways have been erected to facilitate access for passengers with mobility difficulties. (I. Baker)

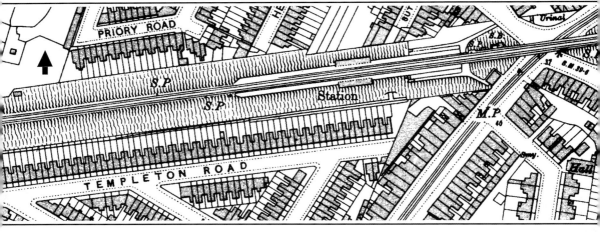

5miles 31chains from St. Pancras stood the station at St. Ann's Road, which opened on 2nd October 1882 and can be seen on this map of 1913. It closed during World War II on 9th August 1942, but the signal box, which was located to the east of the down platform, remained in use until 23rd February 1957.

67.　This view, dating from the late 1940s, looks west from a signal post and shows a freight train passing the disused station at St. Ann's Road, with the brick street level building seen to the left. From this, a ramp led directly to the up platform, whilst a subway beneath the tracks and a further ramp provided access to the down side. Being built almost entirely of wood, the platforms and associated structures left no tangible remains after demolition, in common with the signal box which can be seen on the right. The street level building, however, with a much altered frontage, survived as a shop and the remains of a decapitated lamp post were still evident on one of the approach ramps at the beginning of 2005.　(G. Weller collection)

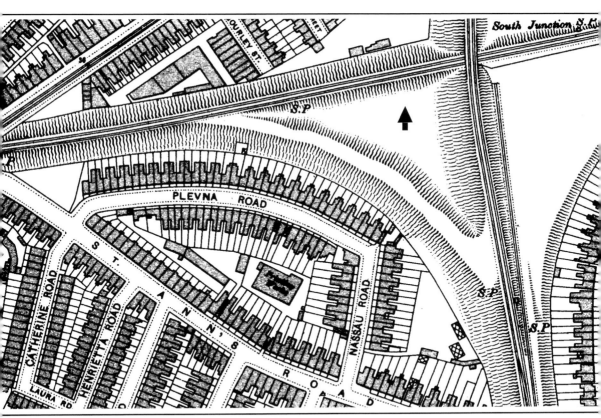

East of St. Ann's Road, a curve was partially constructed to provide a link with the GER Bethnal Green - Edmonton line of 1872, and would have joined it to the north of Stamford Hill station. The scheme was aborted however and the embankment, which can be seen on this map of 1913, was subsequently used as allotments. When the GER line was authorised, other junctions were planned at this point and the alignment of the street to the far right indicates the intended course of the south-east curve. On the map, the THJR runs east to west, whilst the GER stretches from north to south.

SOUTH TOTTENHAM

(map labels) IPPLEPE... N. ROAD · Chap. HIGHWEEK ROAD · STONEBRIDGE ROAD · G.E.R. · SEVEN SISTERS CURVE · S.Ps · TOWNSEND ROAD · F.B. · F.B. · South Tottenham & Stamford Hill Station · B.M. 40 3 · W.P. M.P. · S.P. · S.B. · South Tot... Junct... · Tottenham South Junction · S.Ps · L.B. · S.P. · ...N.D... ROAD

Opened as South Tottenham & Stamford Hill on 1st May 1871, the station was located 5miles 69chains from St. Pancras and served as a terminus for Midland Railway services prior to the advent of the Tottenham & Forest Gate line. It is seen here on the Ordnance Survey map of 1894, along with the connecting spur to Seven Sisters (left) and part of the goods yard (right). This survived until July 1966.

68. To the right of this view from the early twentieth century we see the station's street level building, which may possibly have been a later addition or at least reconstruction. The GER Ways & Works Committee minutes of 1st March 1887 refer to a contract being awarded for a "booking office and waiting room", whilst in October 1910 authority was given for a "booking office extension". After these changes however the building remained largely unaltered for many years, but in recent times conversion into a takeaway food outlet has resulted in it receiving a new frontage. The tram journey is illustrated in the Middleton Press album *Waltham Cross and Edmonton Tramways*. (Commercial postcard / P. Laming collection)

69. Passengers stand on the down platform in the early 1900s as a St. Pancras to Southend train arrives behind LTSR 4-4-2T No. 43 *Great Ilford*. In the distance can be seen the bridge taking the GER Bethnal Green - Enfield line over the Tottenham & Hampstead route. (G.W. Goslin collection)

70. The down side building was constructed largely of brick and was in a different style to its wooden counterpart on the opposite platform. It may therefore have dated from the improvements of 1887 although this cannot be confirmed. The up side shelter, seen on the right survived unaltered for many years, although it suffered minor damage due to a fire on 4th February 1904. In this view, which possibly dates from the 1930s, an LMSR Class 4F 0-6-0 is seen arriving with a train heading towards St. Pancras. (Stations UK)

71.   From the western end of the up platform we see LMSR Fowler Class 3F 0-6-0T No. 7260 plod over the High Road bridge and past one of the station running-in boards with an eastbound freight at an unknown date, possibly the late 1940s. These once ubiquitous loco-motives were found all over the LMSR system and were generally referred to as 'Jinties'. The suffix was deleted from the station name in 1949 and it has remained 'South Tottenham' ever since. (Lens of Sutton Collection)

72.   West of the High Road bridge, the double track connection with Seven Sisters curved sharply towards the north. This opened to goods traffic in 1879 with passengers following on 1st January 1880. Here it is seen in the Spring of 1962 soon after a train from North Woolwich to Palace Gates has departed the station behind ER Class L1 2-6-4T No. 67729. The curve closed to passengers on 7th January 1963 with the cessation of Palace Gates ser-vices and was singled in May 1977. Overhead wiring was subsequently added in 1989 and it reopened to passengers with a restricted service linking Stratford with Enfield Town. (G. Silcock)

73. By the Spring of 1976 when this view was taken, the old platform buildings had been demolished and replaced by new shelters. The signal box at the east end of the up platform dates from 1st July 1894, a few days before passenger services were introduced over the new Tottenham & Forest Gate Railway. Its mechanical lever frame was subsequently replaced by a panel on 23rd May 1977 and it has since been subject to other changes. (G. Larkbey)

74. Embankment subsidence has resulted in the platforms being rebuilt and both have been shortened to accommodate 2-car trains only. Our photograph dates from January 2005 and includes the signal box on the right, which, because of the shortening, is now beyond the platform end. The earlier street level building shown in picture No.70 closed in the 1990s and the entrance was transferred to the north side of the formation. Beyond the platform ends, the tracks serving Barking veer to the left, whilst those to the right provide a connection with the former GER Lea Valley line. (J.L. Crook)

BLACK HORSE ROAD GOODS

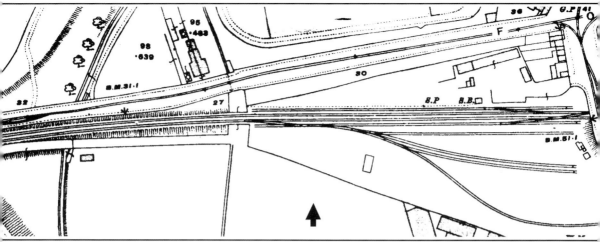

This goods depot was located on the south side of the line, west of Black Horse Road and can be seen to the right of this Ordnance Survey map of 1913. It opened on 1st September 1894 and originally comprised four sidings, which are those shown closest to the passenger tracks. The long curving siding visible towards the base of the map was a later addition, although its date of installation is uncertain. Further enlargement came in April 1917, when three further sidings were laid to the north of the formation, with a connection into the AEC works, which reached the opposite side of Forest Road by means of an un-gated level crossing. This northern section of the yard fell into disuse during the 1950s, but the public goods yard sidings to the south lasted until 7th December 1964, when the yard officially closed. Black Horse Road signal box, which adjoined the down line, was opened on 1st July 1894 and remained in use until 23rd March 1969.

75. The TFGR goods depots do not seem to have been well photographed, so we are lucky to have this delightful view which dates from the early twentieth century. It was taken at Black Horse Road, where the yard was used by coal merchant, Joseph Silk, and shows part of the workforce posing beside the merchant's wagons and horse-drawn carts. (K. Romig collection)

BLACKHORSE ROAD

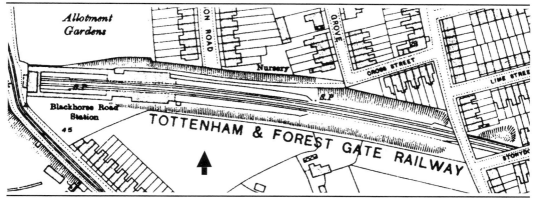

Opened with the Tottenham & Forest Gate line on 9th July 1894, the station was located 7miles 31chains from St. Pancras and 10chains east of the signal box already described. As can be seen from this Ordnance Survey map of 1913, it was entered by way of a street level building on the east side of Black Horse Road, but there was also a footpath connection linking the down platform with Cross Street. Both platforms boasted a length of 500ft and this was a feature shared with the other TFGR stations.

76. Here we see the street level building as it appeared on 14th September 1957, with trolleybus wiring in evidence above. The lower sections on either side of the main structure are thought to have been intended as exits, but that visible on the right had been bricked-up some time prior to the photograph being taken. (H. C. Casserley)

77. A covered footbridge at the rear of the street level building led to two enclosed ramps which provided access to and from the platforms. The base of that serving the down side can be seen in this 1957 view, which looks towards Barking and also includes the footpath link with Cross Street in the middle distance. (H.C. Casserley)

78. We move on to 23rd April 1960 and see ex-LMSR Class 4F 0-6-0 No. 44210 arriving at the down platform with the 12.26pm train from Kentish Town to Southend. In early days, the station name was always shown as 'Black Horse Road', but around the BR period it was sometimes referred to as 'Blackhorse Road' and this is borne out by the differing running-in boards illustrated in these two photographs. (H.C. Casserley)

79. The covered footbridge at the rear of the street level building provided an excellent position for photographers who wanted a general over-view of the station. This picture which shows an eastbound 4-car Cravens' diesel multiple unit standing at the down platform, dates from the early 1960s. (Photographer unknown)

80. Black Horse Road was the last TFGR station to retain its original platform buildings and these survived until the Spring of 1977. By the time this view was taken on 17th April of that year, the down side awning had already been removed and work was under way demolishing the other. Ropes were attached to the canopy bays, then tugged by men on the opposite platform until they crashed onto the track in a cloud of dust. Needless to say trains were not operating at the time! (J. Guy)

81. The old wooden buildings were replaced by a pair of very basic platform shelters, one of which is visible in this view which dates from 16th August 1981. As can be seen, the covering which had previously protected the footbridge and associated ramps had also disappeared, although the booking office at street level continued to stand. The leading car of the DMU is in plain blue livery whilst the others are blue and grey. When re-signed in the BR corporate image style, the nameboards all displayed the title as 'Black Horse Road' and therefore eradicated the earlier anomaly. (D. Pearson)

82.   In order to provide better interchange facilities with Blackhorse Road station on the Victoria Line, it was decided to replace the existing premises with completely new platforms adjoining part of the former goods yard site. This view, taken on 8th November 1981, shows construction in hand, with the footbridge span being lowered into position. (D. Pearson)

83. The original premises closed from 14th December 1981, when their replacement was brought into use on the opposite side of the road. This view, taken from a passing train, shows demolition of the former up platform in progress and the new station beyond the bridge. The old street level building survived until closure, but was demolished soon after. (G. Larkbey)

84. The title of the present station has been 'Blackhorse Road' from the outset and is displayed as such on the nameboards. This view, taken in the early 1990s looks towards Barking. Since resiting, the platforms have been accessed by way of the Underground street level building. (B.P. Pask)

A Through Service of MIDLAND GOODS and COAL TRAINS is established over the TOTTENHAM and FOREST GATE RAILWAY in connection with the TILBURY DEEP WATER DOCKS and Stations on the LONDON, TILBURY, & SOUTHEND RAILWAY.

The London Shipping rates apply to goods for the docks at Tilbury. Direct access to the docks is given by trucks running alongside ships berthed therein.

The undermentioned Goods and Coal Depots, situated on the TOTTENHAM and FOREST GATE RAILWAY are open for Goods and Mineral Traffic, viz., BLACK HORSE ROAD (for Higham Hill, Higham Hill Common, St. James's Street, and Chapel End), QUEEN'S ROAD, WALTHAMSTOW (for Hoe Street, Wood Street, Knotts Green, Whipps Cross, and Walthamstow generally), LEYTON, LEYTONSTONE (for Leytonstone, Wanstead, Stratford New Town, Maryland Point, and Harrow Green).

Enquiries should be addressed to Mr. E. Chalk, Goods Manager, London, Tilbury, and Southend Railway, Fenchurch Street Station, London, E.C. ; or the Midland Company's Agents :—Mr. H. Mason, Tilbury Docks ; Mr. H. McConkey, St. Pancras Station (respecting stations on the Tottenham and Forest Gate Railway); Mr. J. Rawson (Chief City Agent), 13, Aldersgate Street ; or Mr. J. Shaw, Mineral Manager, Midland Railway, Derby ; and Mr. W. E. Adie, Goods Manager, Midland Railway, Derby.

To ensure the traffic travelling by this route Consignment Notes should be endorsed "Per MIDLAND RAILWAY."

Bemrose & Sons, Limited, Derby London and Watford

Cover of a public timetable leaflet from 1902. (K. Romig collection)

WALTHAMSTOW QUEEN'S ROAD

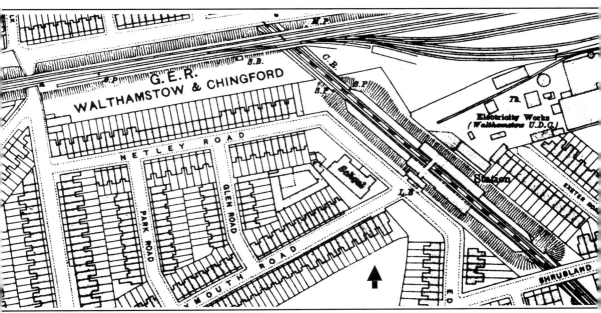

Opened as 'Walthamstow' with the line on 9th July 1894, the station was positioned 8miles 11chains from St. Pancras and can be seen towards the right of this map of 1913. It was originally provided with a signal box at the south-eastern end of the down platform, but this was abolished on 9th August 1903, when it was replaced by a pair of 2-lever open ground frames. The line shown crossing from left to right near the top of the map, together with its adjoining sidings, belonged to the GER and is featured in the Middleton Press publication *Liverpool Street to Chingford*.

85. We start our look at Walthamstow with this view of Stanier Class 4MT 2-6-4T No. 42532 arriving with the 2.30pm train from Kentish Town to Barking on 14th September 1957. Although the nameboards at this time were post-nationalisation replacements, the frames in which they were displayed originally held LMSR 'hawkseye' style signs of the 1930s. (H.C. Casserley)

86. Ex-LMSR Fowler Class 3MT 2-6-2T No. 40036 was fitted with condensing apparatus for working over the Metropolitan City Widened lines and is seen departing from Walthamstow with a train for Barking on 5th December 1959. (E. Wilmshurst)

87. The street level building dated from opening and remained little changed when this view was taken in 1968. To the right we see the covered footbridge which led to the platforms, whilst behind this is a part of the former Walthamstow UDC electricity works. The central doorway and windows served the booking hall, whilst the window to the far left belonged to the station master's office and that to the right, with a protective grille, illuminated the ticket office. The canopy over the station entrance was subsequently removed and the building was demolished in March 1995. (I. Baker)

88. This view shows a Craven's diesel multiple unit, awaiting departure from the up platform whilst working between Barking and Kentish Town in the second half of the 1960s. The station was renamed 'Walthamstow Queen's Road' on 6th May 1968, but underwent no further changes until 1972, when the platform buildings were demolished and footbridge covering was removed. (I. Baker)

89. New shelters were erected following demolition of the platform buildings and one of these is visible to the right of this view which shows a DMU travelling towards Barking. Just beyond the platform ends can be seen the bridge carrying the electrified ex-GER Chingford line, along with one of its catenaries. A footpath linking the down platform with Walthamstow Central on the Chingford route was brought into use in 1992, but was abandoned about six years later when part of its course was redeveloped. (K. Romig)

90. Bo-Bo diesel locomotive No. 33 103 is seen hauling a 3-TC set at Walthamstow Queen's Road on 24th August 1999, after the north-western end of the platforms had fallen into disuse. Although the footbridge lost its covering and received new steps in 1972, the old span was retained along with its cast-iron pillar supports and one of these is just visible to the extreme left. In recent years, facilities have been improved by the addition of sloping access ramps from street level and better platform lighting. (M. Batten)

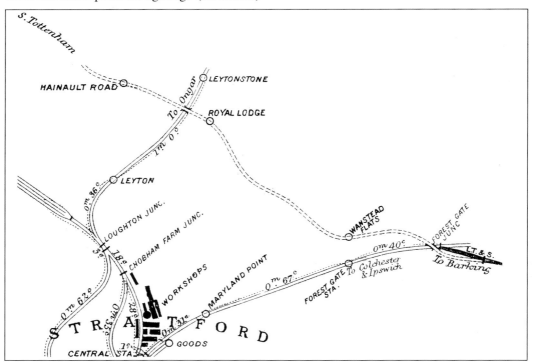

An extract from *Airey's Railway Map of London and its Suburbs* dated 1893, which shows alternative names of the TFGR stations which opened the following year as Leyton, Leytonstone and Wanstead Park. These do not seem to have appeared in any official documents however and were probably included by the cartographer before the actual titles were known. (K. Romig collection)

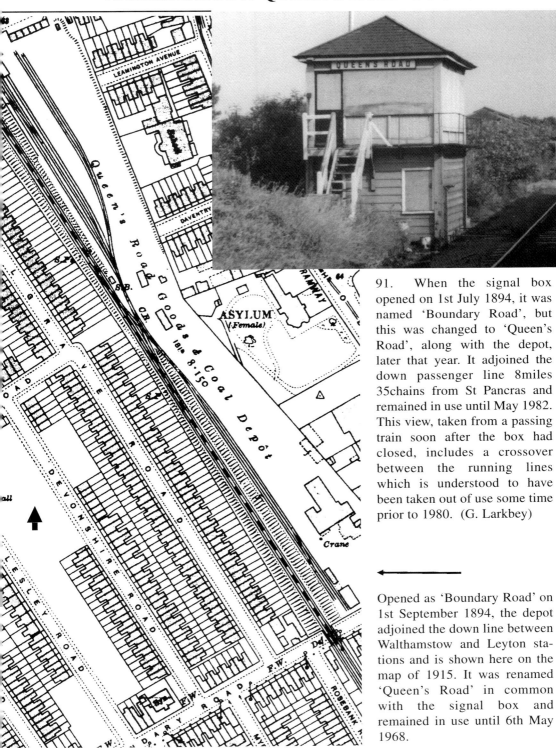

91. When the signal box opened on 1st July 1894, it was named 'Boundary Road', but this was changed to 'Queen's Road', along with the depot, later that year. It adjoined the down passenger line 8miles 35chains from St Pancras and remained in use until May 1982. This view, taken from a passing train soon after the box had closed, includes a crossover between the running lines which is understood to have been taken out of use some time prior to 1980. (G. Larkbey)

Opened as 'Boundary Road' on 1st September 1894, the depot adjoined the down line between Walthamstow and Leyton stations and is shown here on the map of 1915. It was renamed 'Queen's Road' in common with the signal box and remained in use until 6th May 1968.

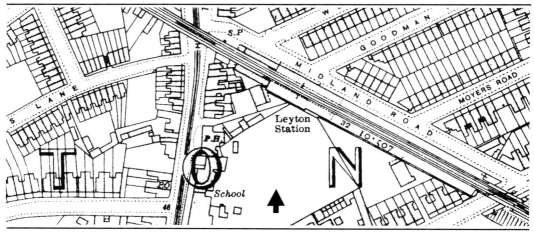

The station, which stood 9miles 22chains from St. Pancras, was opened as 'Leyton' along with the line on 9th July 1894. It was constructed on viaduct and was accessed by means of covered stairways from a street level entrance at its north-western end, as shown on this Ordnance Survey map of 1915. It was renamed Leyton Midland Road on 1st May 1949, but otherwise remained little altered until its facilities were rationalised in the 1970s.

92. From High Road, Leyton we look across and see the station entrance, which was located on the down side of the formation, in Midland Road. The open door, just visible left of centre, beyond the two lorries, led into the booking hall which was accommodated within an arch. Subsequent rationalisation saw the platform buildings and stairway covering removed, and a replacement street level building was provided in the 1980s. This was closed around the end of the following decade and a new entrance was opened on the up side, leading directly onto the High Road. The line was built largely on viaduct from south of Queen's Road to beyond Wanstead Park, but the stretch adjoining Leyton goods depot, including the permanent way hut seen in the distance, was on embankment. (Photographer unknown)

93. This view from the up line looks towards Barking and shows the characteristic wooden buildings which were demolished early in 1971 and subsequently replaced by brick shelters. In the distance, to the right, stands the signal box, which controlled movements around the adjoining goods yard and operated the station signals. This had replaced the original cabin on 19th February 1926 and remained in use until 10th February 1969. (Lens of Sutton Collection)

94. We stand on the up platform in the 1960s and observe Type 2 Bo-Bo No. D5219 passing through the station with a short eastbound freight. (K. Romig)

95.   Moving on to 14th November 1985, we watch a Class 104 DMU arriving at the down platform. These units had previously worked in the Manchester area and operated Gospel Oak - Barking services from the 1980s until the early 1990s. (M. Batten)

96. To mark the centenary of the Tottenham & Forest Gate Railway, the Barking - Gospel Oak Line User Group organised a special excursion to Southend on Sunday 10th July 1994. Here we see passengers joining the train at Leyton Midland Road, which was decorated with banners and balloons to mark the occasion. Near the centre of the view stands one of the brick platform waiting shelters, erected after the original buildings were demolished. (G. Larkbey)

LEYTON MIDLAND ROAD GOODS

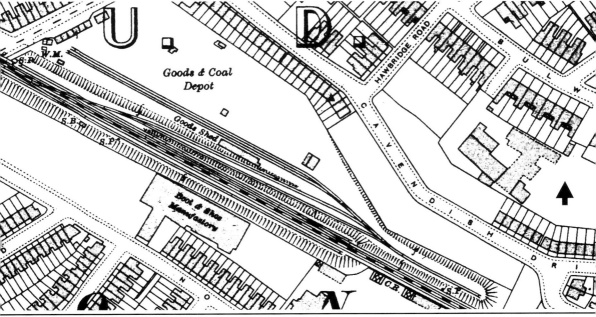

The goods and coal yard at Leyton opened on 1st September 1894 and was located to the south-east of the passenger station. The two public sidings were at street level, requiring a steep incline down from the embankment. Road access was from Hainault Road as shown on the Ordnance Survey map of 1915.

97. No views have been found of the yard itself, but we do have this photograph, dating from 1972, which shows the various coal offices facing onto the south-eastern side of Hainault Road with the depot gate on the right. (I. Baker)

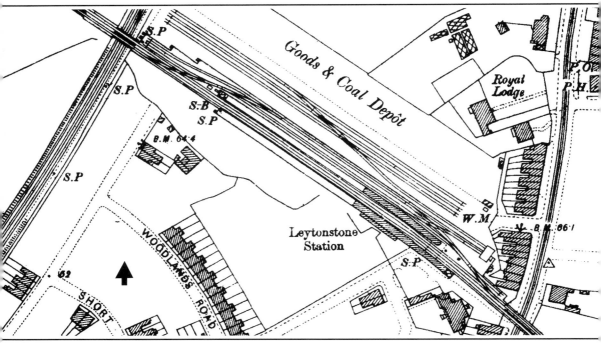

Opened as Leytonstone on 9th July 1894, the passenger station was located 9miles 79chains from St. Pancras. The adjoining goods and coal depot, brought into use on 1st September 1894, was located at street level and was linked to sidings behind the down platform by means of a wagon hoist. This section of the Ordnance Survey map of 1914 also includes the GER Stratford - Ongar line on the left.

98. The street level entrance was rather more elaborate than that at Leyton. This view, which dates from the pre-grouping era, includes a line-up of staff, posing with a milkman, whose small horse-drawn cart is partly visible on the left. (K. Romig collection)

99. The platform buildings were positioned at the Barking end and can be seen in this view which is thought to date from the 1930s. Damage sustained during World War II resulted in the stairway roofs being removed along with adjoining sections of awning. The station was renamed Leytonstone High Road on 1st May 1949, but otherwise remained unaltered well into the next decade. (Stations UK)

100. With the station in such poor condition it was obvious that the original buildings were living on borrowed time and a rebuilding scheme was eventually announced. In this atmospheric view, so typical of the 1950s London railway scene, we see work-stained Fairburn 2-6-4T No. 42686 pausing at the up platform. (R.M. Casserley)

101. The rebuilding of the down side was completed in October 1957, with the up side following soon after. This view looks south-eastward on 28th February 1959 and includes the new buildings and replacement platform lighting. (H.C. Casserley)

102. Turning in the opposite direction, the photographer recorded ex-LMSR Stanier 2-6-2T No. 40100 arriving with the 1.00pm Kentish Town - Barking train. The signal box dated from 1st July 1894 and controlled operations around the station area. The street level goods yard closed, along with the wagon hoist in May 1968, and the connections to the the sidings behind the down passenger platform were taken out of use on 19th February 1969. After this, the box was retained to operate the signals and also the crossover seen in the photograph. The latter was abandoned from 20th February 1994 however and the box, which had not been operational since January 1993, was officially abolished. Surprisingly the signal box nameboard remained unaltered, without the 'High Road' suffix for many years, and it was only towards its final days that a Network SouthEast sign showing the amended title was finally fitted. (H.C. Casserley)

103. A pair of Cravens two-car diesel multiple units coupled together are seen at the down platform, whilst working between Kentish Town and Barking on 13th April 1971. The modern platform buildings which had seemed so smart and stylish in 1957 subsequently fell foul of vandalism
and were demolished in January 1996. (M. Batten)

104. The 1957 buildings were subsequently replaced by small shelters as seen in this photograph which shows a Class 150 DMU heading towards Gospel Oak. The 500ft long platforms
have been effectively shortened by having their western ends fenced off, but the sections still
in use are enlivened by the addition of floral displays thanks to the efforts of the Line User
Group. (J.L. Crook)

WANSTEAD PARK

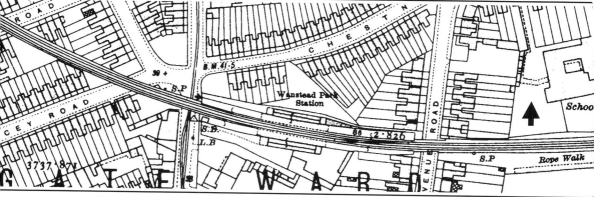

Shown on Airey's map as 'Wanstead Flats' and referred to by the LTSR as 'Forest Gate' prior to opening, Wanstead Park was brought into use on 9th July 1894. It was located 11miles 15chains from St. Pancras and is shown on this Ordnance Survey map of 1915. The station, which was constructed on viaduct, dealt with passenger traffic only and had no goods facilities.

105. From the west end of the up platform we see ex-LMSR Class 4F 0-6-0 No 44529 arriving with the 12.26pm train from Kentish Town to Southend on 28th February 1959. The signal box shown on the left dated from the opening of the line and, in addition to working signals, operated a crossover at the eastern end of the station which became operational in September 1901. This crossover was taken out of use on 19th December 1965 and the box was abolished from the same date. (H.C. Casserley)

106.   Remaining on the up platform we again look west, but the date is now 1968 and the signal box has disappeared. A Cravens DMU has just arrived, but there appears to be very little in the way of passenger activity. To the right, behind the platform gas lamp, we see the top of a covered and glazed stairway which led from the booking hall. (I. Baker)

107.   Moving to the opposite end of the platform on the same occasion, we are rewarded with a clear, unobscured view of the wooden buildings, which were destined to be demolished two years later. (I. Baker)

108. After the platform buildings were removed in 1970, they were replaced by a pair of small brick shelters as shown here. Inside can be seen a section of original bench seating, which was salvaged at the time of demolition. Other changes undertaken around this time included the removal of the stairway roofing and the replacement of the original booking office by one located within a Portakabin. (G. Larkbey)

109. We now see the station as it appeared in early 2005, after the next generation of platform shelter had replaced those of 1970. The view looks east and includes overgrown sections of platform in the distance, which were made redundant by the operation of shorter trains. In recent times new access stairways have been erected which lead to and from the main Woodgrange Road, as opposed to 'Station Approach' as before. (J.L. Crook)

WOODGRANGE PARK

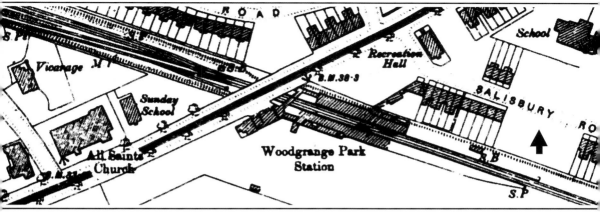

The line between Barking and Forest Gate Junction on what was to become the GER was opened by the London Tilbury & Southend Railway on 13th April 1854, but initially had no intermediate stations. With the advent of the TFGR however, a junction was laid and, to the east of this, a station named Woodgrange Park was brought into use on 9th July 1894. It was located 12miles 3chains from St. Pancras and is shown on this map which dates from its year of opening. Although the passenger station appears to be complete, the sidings subsequently laid to the south of the formation in connection with Woodgrange Park goods depot have yet to be laid. This depot was opened on 1st January 1895 and survived, latterly as a coal depot only, until 7th December 1964. To the left of the map we see the two TFGR tracks below and the connection with the GER above. The latter line lost its regular passenger trains on 1st May 1918, but was reopened on 6th January 1969, when some LTS route trains began running to and from Liverpool Street. The route is featured in *Liverpool Street to Ilford* (Middleton Press)

110. To the right of this early twentieth century view we see the street level building at Woodgrange Park, together with the roof of its covered footbridge. Behind the two ladies walking towards the camera is an additional doorway, which provided direct access to and from the footbridge and is thought to have been used as an exit. (Commercial postcard / P. Laming collection)

111. The platform buildings, which were largely constructed of brick, can be seen in this view dating from the 1950s, which shows Stanier Class 3MT 2-6-2T No. 40160 having just arrived with the 1.00pm from Kentish Town to East Ham. Wagons are evident in the adjoining sidings, but, other than the passenger train, very little appears to be happening in the way of activity. The awnings were removed and their associated buildings demolished during the 1970s, although a truncated section of that on the down side was retained as the platform rear wall. (H.C. Casserley)

112. We move over to the up platform on 20th May 1985 and watch Brush Co-Co No. 47115 passing with a freight train. The signal box seen to the left dated from 1st July 1894 and remained in use until 25th May 1996. AC overhead wiring of the 6.25kV type was installed between Forest Gate Junction and Barking on 6th November 1961 and was converted to 25kV on 22nd May 1988. (M. Batten)

113. Here we see former Southern Region electro-diesel locomotive No. 73106 passing Woodgrange Park on 6th March 1991. On the right is a surviving section of the down side building wall, whilst the covered footbridge, dating from opening, appears above the train. (M. Batten)

114. Brush Co-Co No. 47702 *County of Suffolk* wheels a freight train through the station on 10th October 1996. The footbridge was removed in 1994, and the erstwhile exit doorway on the down side, long-since locked, was brought back into use as a station entrance with new stairs to the down platform. (M. Batten)

EAST HAM

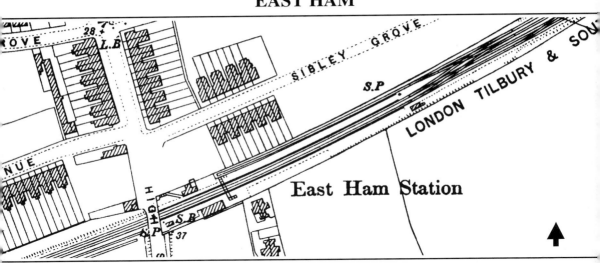

East Ham Station

The Ordnance Survey map of 1894 shows East Ham station before the surrounding area had been completely developed. It was opened by the London Tilbury & Southend Railway on 31st March 1858 and served by TFGR line trains from 9th July 1894. General growth of traffic and the subsequent eastward extension of Metropolitan District Railway services resulted in a widening of the formation and the station being rebuilt with five platform faces between 1902 and 1904.

115. This view, which looks towards Fenchurch Street from the up main line platform, dates from 16th August 1958, when electrification work was in its early stages. To the extreme right we see a train for Kentish Town awaiting departure from the bay which was provided for TFGR services during the 1902-4 rebuilding. (R.M. Casserley)

116. We now have a closer view of a Kentish Town train as it is about to leave the bay at East Ham, headed by ex-LMSR Fowler Class 3MT 2-6-2T No. 40028. The bay closed when the service was withdrawn on 15th September 1958 and its track is thought to have been lifted late in the following month. Elsewhere on the station, the 'Fenchurch Street' side was subject to changes resulting from track re-alignment in 1959 and the 'main line' platforms were taken out of use on 18th June 1962. After this East Ham was served solely by London Transport trains, but the station retained many of its LTSR features. Further views of East Ham appear in the Middleton Press volume *Fenchurch Street to Barking*. (F. Church)

WEST OF BARKING

117. The British Railways Modernisation Plan announced in the mid-1950s brought changes in and around Barking. To improve traffic flow, two flyovers were provided west of the station, of which one was for the use of services travelling to and from the Kentish Town line and the other was for westbound LT trains. This view shows Brush Type 2 A1A-A1A No. D5506 hauling an up freight from the Tilbury direction towards Woodgrange Park, probably soon after this flyover was fully commissioned on 11th May 1959. (British Railways)

BARKING

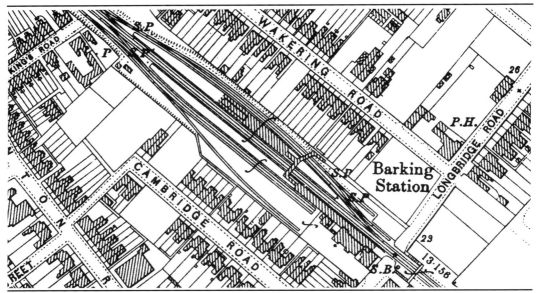

Opened by the LTSR on 13th April 1854 and recorded by the Midland Railway as being located 13miles 53chains from St. Pancras. The station is shown on this map of 1894, together with its adjoining goods yard. Throughout its long history many changes have taken place including a down loop and up bay, which were added in 1889. The level crossings were replaced by bridges in 1906 and, around the same time, the premises were further enlarged.

118.   This view looks east during the early stages of modernisation in 1956, and shows the rear of the street level building which had been erected when the station was enlarged between 1906 and 1908. Just beyond the East Street bridge we can see a train formed of Q Stock, which was then a common sight on the LT District Line. (J.P. Richards)

119. This view looks east on 28th February 1959 and shows a temporary platform which was erected for the use of Kentish Town services whilst the station was being rebuilt. See also the Middleton Press volumes : *Fenchurch Street to Barking*, *Barking to Southend* and *Tilbury Loop*. (H.C. Casserley)

120. The rebuilding of Barking station was officially completed on 29th September 1961. We end our exploration of the route with this 1990s photograph which again looks east and includes a Gospel Oak DMU on the extreme left with an eastbound District Line train standing at the adjoining platform face. (G. Larkbey)

MP Middleton Press

EVOLVING THE ULTIMATE RAIL **ENCYCLOPEDIA**

Easebourne Lane, Midhurst, West Sussex.
GU29 9AZ Tel:01730 813169

www.middletonpress.co.uk email:info@middletonpress.co.uk
A-0 906520 B-1 873793 C-1 901706 D-1 904474

OOP Out of Print at time of printing - Please check current availability **BROCHURE AVAILABLE SHOWING NEW TITLES**

A
Abergavenny to Merthyr C 91 5
Aldgate & Stepney Tramways B 70 7
Allhallows - Branch Line to A 62 2
Alton - Branch Lines to A 11 8
Andover to Southampton A 82 7
Ascot - Branch Lines around A 64 9
Ashburton - Branch Line to B 95 2
Ashford - Steam to Eurostar B 67 7
Ashford to Dover A 48 7
Austrian Narrow Gauge D 04 7
Avonmouth - BL around D 42 X
B
Banbury to Birmingham D 27 6
Barking to Southend C 80 X
Barnet & Finchley Tramways B 93 6
Barry - Branch Lines around D 50 0
Basingstoke to Salisbury A 89 4
Bath Green Park to Bristol C 36 2
Bath to Evercreech Junction A 60 6
Bath Tramways B 86 3
Battle over Portsmouth 1940 A 29 0
Battle over Sussex 1940 A 79 7
Bedford to Wellingborough D 31 4
Betwixt Petersfield & Midhurst A 94 0
Blitz over Sussex 1941-42 B 35 9
Bodmin - Branch Lines around B 83 9
Bognor at War 1939-45 B 59 6
Bombers over Sussex 1943-45 B 51 0
Bournemouth & Poole Trys B 47 2
Bournemouth to Evercreech Jn A 46 0
Bournemouth to Weymouth A 57 6
Bournemouth Trolleybuses C 10 9
Bradford Trolleybuses D 19 5
Brecon to Neath D 43 8
Brecon to Newport D 16 0
Brickmaking in Sussex B 19 7
Brightons Tramways B 02 2 OOP
Brighton to Eastbourne A 16 9
Brighton to Worthing A 03 7
Brighton Trolleybuses D 34 9
Bristols Tramways B 57 X
Bristol to Taunton D 03 9
Bromley South to Rochester B 23 5
Bude - Branch Line to B 29 4
Burnham to Evercreech Jn A 68 1
Burton & Ashby Tramways C 51 6
C
Camberwell & West Norwood Tys B 22 7
Cambridge to Ely D 55 1
Canterbury - Branch Lines around B 58 8
Cardiff Trolleybuses D 64 0
Caterham & Tattenham Corner B 25 1
Changing Midhurst C 15 X
Chard and Yeovil - BLs around C 30 3
Charing Cross to Dartford A 75 4
Charing Cross to Orpington A 96 7
Cheddar - Branch Line to B 90 1
Cheltenham to Andover C 43 5
Chesterfield Tramways D 37 3
Chesterfield Trolleybuses D 51 9
Chichester to Portsmouth A 14 2
Clapham & Streatham Trys B 97 9 OOP
Clapham Junction - 50 yrs C 06 0 OOP
Clapham Junction to Beckenham Jn B 36 7
Clevedon & Portishead - BLs to D 18 7
Collectors Trains, Trolleys & Trams D 29 2
Colonel Stephens D62 4
Cornwall Narrow Gauge D 56 X
Crawley to Littlehampton A 34 7
Cromer - Branch Lines around C 26 5
Croydons Tramways B 42 1
Croydons Trolleybuses B 73 1 OOP
Croydon to East Grinstead B 48 0
Crystal Palace (HL) & Catford Loop A 87 8
D
Darlington Trolleybuses D 33 0
Dartford to Sittingbourne B 34 0
Derby Tramways D 17 9
Derby Trolleybuses C 72 9
Derwent Valley - Branch Line to the D 06 3
Didcot to Banbury D 02 0
Didcot to Swindon C 84 2
Didcot to Winchester C 13 3
Douglas to Peel C 88 5
Douglas to Port Erin C 55 9
Douglas to Ramsey D 39 X
Dover's Tramways B 24 3
Dover to Ramsgate A 78 9

E
Ealing to Slough C 42 7
Eastbourne to Hastings A 27 4
East Cornwall Mineral Railways D 22 5
East Croydon to Three Bridges A 53 3
East Grinstead - Branch Lines to A 07 X
East Ham & West Ham Tramways B 52 9
East Kent Light Railway A 61 4
East London - Branch Lines of C 44 3
East London Line B 80 4
East Ridings Secret Resistance D 21 7
Edgware & Willesden Tramways C 18 4
Effingham Junction - BLs around A 74 6
Eltham & Woolwich Tramways B 74 X
Ely to Kings Lynn C 53 2
Ely to Norwich C 90 7
Embankment & Waterloo Tramways B 41 3
Enfield & Wood Green Trys C 03 6 OOP
Enfield Town & Palace Gates - BL to D 32 2
Epsom to Horsham A 30 4
Euston to Harrow & Wealdstone C 89 3
Exeter & Taunton Tramways B 32 4
Exeter to Barnstaple B 15 4
Exeter to Newton Abbot C 49 4
Exeter to Tavistock B 69 3
Exmouth - Branch Lines to B 00 6
F
Fairford - Branch Line to A 52 5
Falmouth, Helston & St. Ives - BL to C 74 5
Fareham to Salisbury A 67 3
Faversham to Dover B 05 7 OOP
Felixstowe & Aldeburgh - BL to D 20 9
Fenchurch Street to Barking C 20 6
Festiniog - 50 yrs of enterprise C 83 4
Festiniog in the Fifties B 68 5
Festiniog in the Sixties B 91 X
Finsbury Park to Alexandra Palace C 02 8
Frome to Bristol B 77 4
Fulwell - Trams, Trolleys & Buses D 11 X
G
Gloucester to Bristol D 35 7
Gloucester to Cardiff D 66 7
Gosport & Horndean Trys B 92 8
Gosport - Branch Lines around A 36 3
Great Yarmouth Tramways D 13 6
Greenwich & Dartford Tramways B 14 6 OOP
Guildford to Redhill A 63 0
H
Hammersmith & Hounslow Trys C 33 8
Hampshire Narrow Gauge D 36 5
Hampshire Waterways A 84 3 OOP
Hampstead & Highgate Tramways B 53 7
Harrow to Watford D 14 4
Hastings to Ashford A 37 1 OOP
Hastings Tramways B 18 9 OOP
Hastings Trolleybuses B 81 2 OOP
Hawkhurst - Branch Line to A 66 5
Hayling - Branch Line to A 12 6
Haywards Heath to Seaford A 28 2
Henley, Windsor & Marlow - BL to C77 X
Hereford to Newport D 54 3
Hitchin to Peterborough D 07 1
Holborn & Finsbury Tramways B 79 0
Holborn Viaduct to Lewisham A 81 9
Horsham - Branch Lines to A 02 9
Huddersfield Trolleybuses C 92 3
Hull Tramways D60 8
Hull Trolleybuses D 24 1
Huntingdon - Branch Lines around A 93 2
I
Ilford & Barking Tramways B 61 8
Ilford to Shenfield C 97 4
Ilfracombe - Branch Line to B 21 9
Ilkeston & Glossop Tramways D 40 3
Industrial Rlys of the South East A 09 6
Ipswich to Saxmundham C 41 9
Ipswich Trolleybuses D 59 4
Isle of Wight Lines - 50 yrs C 12 5
K
Kent & East Sussex Waterways A 72 X
Kent Narrow Gauge C 45 1
Kingsbridge - Branch Line to C 98 2
Kingston & Hounslow Loops A 83 5
Kingston & Wimbledon Tramways B 56 1
Kingswear - Branch Line to C 17 6
L
Lambourn - Branch Line to C 70 2
Launceston & Princetown - BL to C 19 2
Lewisham & Catford Tramways B 26 X OOP
Lewisham to Dartford A 92 4

Lines around Wimbledon B 75 8
Liverpool Street to Chingford D 01 2
Liverpool Street to Ilford C 34 6
Liverpool Tramways - Eastern C 04 4
Liverpool Tramways - Northern C 46 X
Liverpool Tramways - Southern C 23 0
London Bridge to Addiscombe B 20 0
London Bridge to East Croydon A 58 4
London Chatham & Dover Railway A 88 6
London Termini - Past and Proposed D 00 4
London to Portsmouth Waterways B 43 X
Longmoor - Branch Lines to A 41 X
Looe - Branch Line to C 22 2
Lyme Regis - Branch Line to A 45 2
Lynton - Branch Line to B 04 9
M
Maidstone & Chatham Tramways B 40 5
Maidstone Trolleybuses C 00 1 OOP
March - Branch Lines around B 09 X
Margate & Ramsgate Tramways C 52 4
Marylebone to Rickmansworth D49 7
Midhurst - Branch Lines around A 49 5
Midhurst - Branch Lines to A 01 0 OOP
Military Defence of West Sussex A 23 1
Military Signals, South Coast C 54 0
Minehead - Branch Line to A 80 0
Mitcham Junction Lines B 01 4
Mitchell & company C 59 1
Moreton-in-Marsh to Worcester D 26 8
Moretonhampstead - Branch Line to C 27 3
N
Newbury to Westbury C 66 4
Newport (IOW) - Branch Lines to A 26 6
Newquay - Branch Lines to C 71 0
Newton Abbot to Plymouth C 60 5
Northern France Narrow Gauge C 75 3
North East German Narrow Gauge D 44 6
North Kent Tramways B 44 8
North London Line B 94 4
North Woolwich - BLs around C 65 6
Norwich Tramways C 40 0
Nottinghamshire & Derbyshire T/B D 63 2
Nottinghamshire & Derbyshire T/W D 53 5
O
Orpington to Tonbridge B 03 0
Oxford to Bletchley D57 8
Oxford to Moreton-in-Marsh D 15 2
P
Paddington to Ealing C 37 0
Paddington to Princes Risborough C 81 8
Padstow - Branch Line to B 54 5
Plymouth - BLs around B 98 7
Plymouth to St. Austell C 63 X
Pontypool to Mountain Ash D 65 9
Porthmadog 1954-94 - BL around B 31 6
Porthmadog to Blaenau B 50 2 OOP
Portmadoc 1923-46 - BL around B 13 8
Portsmouths Tramways B 72 3 OOP
Portsmouth to Southampton A 31 2
Portsmouth Trolleybuses C 73 7
Princes Risborough - Branch Lines to D 05 5
Princes Risborough to Banbury C 85 0
R
Railways to Victory C 16 8/7 OOP
Reading to Basingstoke B 27 8
Reading to Didcot C 79 6
Reading to Guildford A 47 9 OOP
Reading Tramways B 87 1
Reading Trolleybuses C 05 2
Redhill to Ashford A 73 8
Return to Blaenau 1970-82 C 64 8
Rickmansworth to Aylesbury D 61 6
Roman Roads of Hampshire D 67 5
Roman Roads of Surrey C 61 3
Roman Roads of Sussex C 48 6
Romneyrail C 32 X
Ryde to Ventnor A 19 3
S
Salisbury to Westbury B 39 1
Salisbury to Yeovil B 06 5
Saxmundham to Yarmouth C 69 9
Saxony Narrow Gauge D 47 0
Seaton & Eastbourne Tramways B 76 6
Seaton & Sidmouth - Branch Lines to A 95 9
Secret Sussex Resistance B 82 0
SECR Centenary album C 11 7
Selsey - Branch Line to A 04 5
Sheerness - Branch Lines around B 16 2
Shepherds Bush to Uxbridge T/Ws C 28 1
Shrewsbury - Branch Lines to A 86 X

Sierra Leone Narrow Gauge D 28 4
Sittingbourne to Ramsgate A 90 8
Slough to Newbury C 56 7
Solent - Creeks, Crafts & Cargoes D 52 7
Southamptons Tramways B 33 2 OOP
Southampton to Bournemouth A 42 8
Southend-on-Sea Tramways B 28 6
Southern France Narrow Gauge C 47 8
Southwark & Deptford Tramways B 38 3
Southwold - Branch Line to A 15 0
South Eastern & Chatham Railways C 0X
South London Line B 46 4
South London Tramways 1903-33 D 10 1
St. Albans to Bedford D 08 X
St. Austell to Penzance C 67 2
St. Pancras to Barking D 68 3
St. Pancras to St. Albans C 78 8
Stamford Hill Tramways B 85 5
Steaming through Cornwall B 30 8
Steaming through Kent A 13 4 OOP
Steaming through the Isle of Wight A 56 8
Steaming through West Hants A 69 X
Stratford-upon-Avon to Cheltenham C 2
Strood to Paddock Wood B 12 X
Surrey Home Guard C 57 5
Surrey Narrow Gauge C 87 7
Surrey Waterways A 51 7 OOP
Sussex Home Guard C 24 9
Sussex Narrow Gauge C 68 0
Sussex Shipping Sail, Steam & Motor D 2
Swanley to Ashford B 45 6
Swindon to Bristol C 96 6
Swindon to Gloucester D46 2
Swindon to Newport D 30 6
Swiss Narrow Gauge C 94 X
T
Talyllyn - 50 years C 39 7
Taunton to Barnstaple B 60 X
Taunton to Exeter C 82 6
Tavistock to Plymouth B 88 X
Tees-side Trolleybuses D 58 6
Tenterden - Branch Line to A 21 5
Thanet's Tramways B 11 1 OOP
Three Bridges to Brighton A 35 5
Tilbury Loop C 86 9
Tiverton - Branch Lines around C 62 1
Tivetshall to Beccles D 41 1
Tonbridge to Hastings A 44 4
Torrington - Branch Lines to B 37 5
Tunbridge Wells - Branch Lines to A 32 0
Twickenham & Kingston Trys C 35 4
Two-Foot Gauge Survivors C 21 4 OOP
U
Upwell - Branch Line to B 64 2
V
Victoria & Lambeth Tramways B 49 9
Victoria to Bromley South A 98 3
Victoria to East Croydon A 40 1
Vivarais C 31 1
W
Walthamstow & Leyton Tramways B 65 X
Waltham Cross & Edmonton Trys C 07 9X
Wandsworth & Battersea Tramways B 6.
Wantage - Branch Line to D 25 X
Wareham to Swanage - 50 yrs D 09 8
War on the Line A 10 X
War on the Line VIDEO + 88 0
Waterloo to Windsor A 54 1
Waterloo to Woking A 38 X
Watford to Leighton Buzzard D 45 4
Wenford Bridge to Fowey C 09 5
Westbury to Bath B 55 3
Westbury to Taunton C 76 1
West Cornwall Mineral Railways D 48 9
West Croydon to Epsom B 08 1
West London - Branch Lines of C 50 8
West London Line B 84 7
West Sussex Waterways A 24 X
West Wiltshire - Branch Lines of D 12 8
Weymouth - Branch Lines around A 65 7
Willesden Junction to Richmond B 71 5
Wimbledon to Beckenham C 58 3
Wimbledon to Epsom B 62 6
Wimborne - Branch Lines around A 97 5
Wisbech - Branch Lines around C 01 X
Wisbech 1800-1901 C 93 1
Woking to Alton A 59 2
Woking to Portsmouth A 25 8
Woking to Southampton A 55 X
Woolwich & Dartford Trolleys B 66 9 OO
Worcester to Hereford D 38 1
Worthing to Chichester A 06 1
Y
Yeovil - 50 yrs change C 38 9
Yeovil to Dorchester A 76 2 OOP
Yeovil to Exeter A 91 6